LISTEN

How To Hear God's Voice (better)

By Paul Tubach, Jr.

LISTEN

"LISTEN" by Paul B. Tubach, Jr. is licensed under a Creative Commons Attribution-NonCommercial-NoDerivatives 4.0 International License

You are free to copy, share and redistribute the material in any medium, format or language as long as the text and content is not altered or misconstrued. Freely it was received… freely it is given. The licensor cannot revoke these freedoms as long as you follow these license terms:

- **Attribution** — You must give appropriate credit, provide a link to the website, and indicate if any changes were made. You may do so in any reasonable manner, but not in any way that suggests the author endorses you or your use. "Attribute this work" as: Paul Tubach, Jr., www.newearthministries.org.
- **NonCommercial** — You may not use the material for commercial purposes, i.e. not for any private, corporate, nonprofit or otherwise financial gain.
- **NoDerivatives** — If you remix, transform or build upon the material, you may not distribute the modified material. The creation or development of any derivatives, secondary workbooks or manuals from this book is reserved solely by the author.
- **No additional restrictions** — You may not apply legal terms or technological measures that legally restrict others from doing anything the license permits.

Paperback ISBN 978-1-949892-05-5
Library of Congress Number - pending
Produced in the United States of America
New Earth Ministries

Scriptures taken from the New King James Version. Copyright © 1982 by Thomas Nelson. Used by permission. All rights reserved.

Books and other materials are available online through www.newearthministries.org.

March 2018

Table of Contents

Introduction	xiii
Listen	1
Created To Hear	3
Five Basis Questions	4
Can You Hear God's Voice	6
Who Can Hear	6
Why Do We Want To Hear	9
Be Still and Know This	9
A True Story	12
Keep It Simple	14
Terms	16
The Process of Hearing, Believing	20
How To Listen	22
Hear Him!	25
My Journey To Hear	26
Show Me Your Way	28
Hearing Basics	30
How Do We Silence The Enemy	33
Three Simple Steps	36
Quiet Your Restless Mind	44
One Final Step	51
Other Steps to Hearing	51
Ears For Ministry	52
Be Ready To Listen	54
To Listen Anew	57
Ginosko and Oida	64
Hear The Voice	66
The Conversation	73
Words Of A Similar Meaning	77
Final Authority	80

Hear To Believe	84
"Who" We Listen To	84
A Failure To Communicate	93
Just Tell Us Plainly	97
See What May Come	99
Eyes Of Our Heart	101
Ears Of Our Mind	107
A Time For Understanding	116
Hardened Hearts	119
Reasons Why We Cannot Hear	123
Another Reason	124
Hardened Hearts, Part II	132
What Is a Hardened Heart?	134
Riding a Dead Horse	143
An "other" Reason	145
Created To Hear God's Rhema	146
Origin and Source	148
John 1:1	152
Logos Words To Hear	154
Truth Written On Heart Tablets	159
Conversion Happens	165
Oneness of Hearing	167
The Primary Mission of Jesus	168
Two-Way Journaling	171
Patience in Silence	174
Listening for Spiritual Leaders	179

Appendix

25 ways To Ride A Dead Horse	191

The Image Bearer Series

2. Listen – How To Hear God's Voice – better
3. Image – The Revelation Of God Himself
4. Dominion – Our Heavenly Mandate To Occupy Earth
5. Understand – What Jesus Wants You To Know – and Why
6. Commission – Created On Purpose For A Purpose
7. Gateways – Manifesting Heaven In The Midst Of Chaos
8. Here – The Kingdom Of Heaven Is

The Image Bearer Series is based upon Genesis 1:26-28: "Let us make man in Our image, according to Our likeness… and grant them dominion."

"Image" explains 'who' the Lord of Heaven and Earth is, "Understand" explains 'why' we are here, "Commission" explains 'what' man is and 'how' we were created by the Lord, "Dominion" explains 'what' we are supposed to be doing, "Gateways" explains 'how' we are to accomplish our earthly mission, and "Here" explains our eternal destination is actually – Earth.

Many tools were given to mankind that enables us to accomplish our mission objective to have dominion over the kingdom of darkness – and we need to comprehend this truth: earth is our 'Here' – and our 'when' is now! How God created us – and why – is directly related to our sanctification and accomplishing our multifaceted mission for being on earth.

Why are you here – and what's your purpose in life? These books will answer those questions.

When I began writing in August 2012, four drafts were completed within a year, then on Sept. 27, 2013, the Lord spoke to me and said: "You are My writer. Now write!" and then the Spirit directed me to finish draft #4 which became the initial book, "*Regenesis: A Sojourn To Remember Who We Are*," released in August 2014. Next, the Spirit directed me to work on draft #3 (in reverse order) and then, on October 24, the Spirit told me, "That is not one book with seven chapters – those are seven books." Thus, I have been writing the Image Bearer series under His anointing by hearing His voice and writing what I am directed to write.

Regenesis helped us discover man's true identity, as spiritual beings that are having a human experience, who were created good and upright by God "in His Own image according to His likeness" (Gen. 1:26-27), whereby we have been blessed with many wonderful grace attributes by the Lord to accomplish all that He purposed for man... since the beginning.

Yet for most of us, we've forgotten who we are... and we've forgotten what we are supposed to be doing. Regenesis reminds us who we are, and now, the Image Bearer series is reminding us what we are supposed to do, how we should do it – and more importantly "why" we are doing it.

The Image Bearer series builds upon that knowledge of truth that mankind was created good so as to become what we were created for: to bear His image and imitate Jesus in every respect according to His earthly example – and operate as His heavenly ambassadors for earth.

*** The heavenly pattern for mankind is: imitate Jesus.***
*** The earthly pattern for this world is: become like heaven.***

Who you are is not based upon what you do; "what you do" is based upon "who you are." We get our identity from Jesus. This realigned perspective regarding "who" we are ... is to reorient the applecart of faith pointing in the right direction, to focus on Jesus, and to accomplish our primary mission: have dominion on earth – in the name of Jesus.

The numeric order in which the Spirit directed these books: 1,2,8,3,5,4,6,7 was not linear in the least. Let the Spirit guide you in the order He wants you to read them; however, learning how to "Hear God's Voice" is always mission critical to get started on His path for anyone.

On October 24, 2015, the Lord told me to put these books on the internet for free. This was unexpected, and then the Lord whispered to me, "Can you make money on My words? Freely you have received… freely give."

When the Lord tells you what to do, He will also give you His authority, with power and provision, to do all that He commands. We need to embrace this perspective regarding our life on earth in order to understand and comprehend who we are and what we are supposed to be doing. There is much joy and peace living in this manner, and yet… we all make this choice daily to live according to His purpose for His glory – or to live according to our best laid plans. If I can do it – so can you.

Jesus did it, and therefore – "As He is, so are we in this world" (1 John 4:17). I hope you enjoy the Image Bearer series. Grace and peace be yours in abundance.

It's all about Jesus – and God gets the glory!

Glossary of Terms and Definitions

These are some keys to help navigate and understand the scriptures.

Heaven – God's throne, God's home and the permanent place where God's glory dwells
heaven – the spiritual reality of God's kingdom and Christ's presence upon earth
Glory – the fullness of God's presence; the fullness of all God is
Shekinah Glory – the manifest presence of God's Spirit
Christ – the manifest expression of God in Jesus, and regenerate (born anew) men
Jesus – the manifested Living God; Lord of heaven and earth; Lord of Glory; Lord of Hosts
Host – army (a very important term omitted in the NIV and some other versions)
Host of heaven – angels; sons of God and our heavenly brethren (Rev. 19:10)
Host of earth – sons of men, becoming sons of God in the regeneration
Man – the generic term for male and female to connote mankind, humanity, etc.
Earth – the planet; one of three permanent places within the kingdom of God
Hell – the absence of God; one of three permanent places within the kingdom of God; the pit
World – temporary realm on earth under the dominion and operational control of Satan
Satan – Prince of "this world" (formerly known as Lucifer before he rebelled and fell to earth)
Sin – the operating system of this world in opposition to God's sovereignty; separation from God; things done that cause separation
Spirit – the operating system on earth under the Lord's dominion; the Holy Spirit; God's Spirit
Grace – attributes of God's character that are freely given to man

Light – a metaphor implying God's truth
Darkness – a metaphor implying evil – and sinful lies of "this world"
Wickedness – taking credit for what God has done
Evil – using God's glory and power to accomplish your personal agenda
Paradigm – the operating systems of sin or "by the Spirit" on earth
Paradise – the earthly realm in oneness with God apart from sin
Dwelling – a temporary place to live
Abode – a permanent place to live (of existence)
Rest – the permanent state of being where God's presence abides (in your heart and in heaven)
Kingdom of God – all places under the authority of Jesus
Kingdom of heaven – a term used exclusively in the gospel of Matthew to describe the kingdom of God as it pertains to earth under the Lordship of Jesus Christ

- Life – the source from which all creation exists, and is made alive, as coming from God through Christ Jesus, who is "the Life" and the "author and finisher" of faith (John 14:6; Heb. 12:2)
- Living – those persons spiritually alive with life, who no longer operate in the shadow of Death while sojourning in earthen vessels that will eventually perish for lack of life
- Alive – the spiritual state of being in existence from God's perspective, even apart from the body, and abiding eternally in communion with God's Presence and Spirit
- Dead – the spiritual state of being in existence from God's perspective, but temporarily separated from Him; the eventual disposition of the earthen body without life
- Death – the spiritual state of being permanently and eternally separated from God; the temporary holding place of unregenerate dead that wait there until the judgment

Introduction

God created everyone with the ability to hear His voice, so in one respect, the original subtitle was a misnomer. A better subtitle is… How To Hear God's Voice *Better*.

This book will answer these questions: What does God's voice sound like? What is the single greatest problem preventing us from hearing the Voice that says "I love you"? How can we silence the multitude of many voices? What is the message God wants us to understand?

When we get quiet, become still, and silence all the competing messages and voices in this world, and then focus our attention on Jesus… you will hear God's voice!

Perhaps the single greatest human tragedy is that God hears all our prayers, but we cannot hear His answer. When this happens, we typically proceed to step two, which is the second greatest tragedy: asking other people what God thinks. Man has become quite content with second-hand truth, but this was never God's intent.

If you want to know the truth… then go to the Source… and ask Him yourself.

If you want to hear – then you *WILL* hear! The problem, it seems, is not God's ability to speak to us, but our willingness to listen. We are living in the most exciting time in human history and, yet, this world is coming against us faster and louder with more messages that prevents us from listening for and hearing God's voice.

There are two kingdoms on this planet and they are in conflict with one another. If you want to escape the kingdom of darkness and death to live in the kingdom of love, light and life, then you need to tune into the language of heaven – and hear the truth. There is a way of escape – just listen to Jesus, follow Him, and He will deliver you from darkness. And since Jesus is the Truth and the Life, we need to listen to His Truth, obey His instruction, and understand His message of salvation.

> "See to it that you do not refuse Him who is speaking to you" (Heb. 12:25).

Listen

Listening is the state of being ready to hear.

> Not all who listen will hear…
> but all who truly desire to hear…
> will do whatever it takes to hear His voice!

> "Blessed is the man that hears Me, watching daily at My gates, waiting at the posts of My doors. For whoso finds Me finds life, and shall obtain favor of the Lord" (Proverbs 8:34-35).

Listening to hear God's voice is perhaps the most uniquely identifiable way to know if you are a true follower of Jesus Christ and a faithful believer in the Way. Jesus said:

> ***"My sheep hear My voice, and I know them, and they follow Me" (John 10:27).***

It also comes with this guarantee… "And I give them eternal life" (v. 28). We may claim to know Jesus and we may claim that Jesus knows us, but if we cannot hear His voice, then how do we really know if we have a personal relationship with Him – or whose voice we are listening to – or if our salvation is secure?

Since our salvation is dependent upon hearing His voice, then how can we profess being saved if we cannot hear His voice? Indeed… we cannot!

We live in a world of many voices. Centuries ago, the number of voices that influenced our lives was very limited to a handful, but today – there are thousands of voices that bombard us with thoughts and ideas everywhere we turn. Communication is an important aspect of humanity, but the multitude of voices coming at us in this generation have negatively affected our ability to hear the One True Voice that we need to listen to above all other voices: Jesus Christ.

So, how do we know what His voice sounds like and how can we discern His voice as uniquely identifiable so that we may listen to Him? Well, that is the purpose of this book which will teach you that hearing His voice is not a sound that you hear with the audible hearing of the ears, but with the audible listening of the inner man whose heart and mind operate in spiritual oneness in order to be drawn into a more intimate relationship with God.

The heart and mind hear truth differently – and spiritual truth is no different. The one advantage to hearing God's voice and having a divine two-way conversation with Him is that it does not need to be audible (spoken aloud). The Lord hears all our thoughts… even when we do not think He is listening, *He hears all of them*! So then, there is no reason to speak to God or to hear Him with the mouth or the ears, and it is much preferable to remain this way within the realm of spiritual thought language for this reason: no one else but God can hear our thoughts and prayers.

Why is this so important? Because there are other people and spiritual realities that are listening to our audible voices. When we speak audibly, we become just another one of the many voices within a multitude of many listeners; if our spiritual enemy can hear our voice, then they can influence us with ungodly thoughts in response to our spoken words (which are often contradictory). The darkness of this world is all around us, but the enemy cannot hear our thought language; they can hear our spoken words and they can interpret our outward language and physical expressions, but they cannot hear our thoughts – which becomes a spiritual advantage to us in a world of many voices.

However, we can hear them and this, then, becomes their principle manner whereby they attack us with lies, deception and unbelief. Listening becomes even more complicated when we pray aloud to the Lord because the enemy wants to speak lies to us – and our audible prayers enable them to answer us with deceptively accurate lies veiled as heavenly-sent truth. If we cannot discern the Lord's voice, then we cannot know for certain "from whom" the spiritual voice is coming, and we may be easily fooled by many counterfeit lies from the enemy.

For this reason, Jesus told us to pray in the secret place, which is silently within your inner man (your soul/ mind) within your earthly tabernacle/house/body. Your heavenly Father (and Jesus) will always hear your thoughts offered up in prayer – but the enemy cannot!

The key to hearing God's voice is simple: eliminate the many voices, which include those of your own, so keep your words few. The divine conversation is within the realm of "thought."

Many times I have received answer to prayer and received spiritual wisdom and understanding from the Lord – as His thoughts in response to my thoughts – without the utterance of any words! If no one else knows what I prayed or knows my thoughts because I have not uttered them aloud, then the only possible source for this wisdom and understanding in direct response to my thoughts… is from the Lord.

God is in heaven and you are on the earth, therefore… let your words be few. God is speaking to us all the time – and now it's time for us to turn our hearts attention and affection to Jesus so that we may hear His voice… and follow Him in spirit and in truth.

> "Do not be rash with your mouth, and let not your heart utter anything hastily before God. For God is in heaven, and you on earth; therefore let your words be few" (Eccl. 5:2).

Created To Hear

The Lord created us as image bearers – and His purpose and plan is to give us dominion over the earth. There is a critical step following creation and dominion; it is commission. However, before we are able to understand our purpose as image bearers and the Lord's plan to give us a commission, we must talk about the most important thing about being a follower of Jesus Christ: listening.

> "For who, having heard, rebelled?" (Heb. 3:16)

Jesus wants to have a conversation with us. This sounds so simple, and yet, the most important thing we will ever do as human beings who want to have a personal relationship with Jesus Christ, is simply this: hear Him. Well, of course we are listening, but… can we "hear" His voice?

> "Incline your ear, and come to Me. *Hear*, and your soul shall live" (Isa. 55:3).

Five Basic Questions:

1. Why do we want to listen? Because, deep down, we know that there is something more. Man is forever searching for the missing piece and man is listening to understand one thing – why.

2. How do we even know there is a voice? Because our soul can hear it and it yearns to hear. There is an inner drive and compulsion to dig deeper, to strain to hear the Voice with hope.

3. What does God's voice sound like? You've already heard it – you just didn't know that it was God speaking to you.

4. How can I tell it is God's voice and not some other voice? We will get to that soon enough.

5. Why does God want to talk to us? Because He wants to maintain a personal relationship with us that moves beyond the simple knowing about Him into a complete comprehending of Him in a real, tangible, personal and experiential way.

Know this: everyone can hear God's voice because He is speaking to us all the time. So, if God wants to talk to you, then all He has to do is talk and you will hear Him, right? Well, the Lord has been talking, but our ears may not be ready or prepared to hear Him. If you are expecting to hear an audible voice from God, then you are just like billions of us who desire this to happen, but I know of only a few instances where this has happened in the scriptures – or in real life. So, how does God choose to talk to us? For most of us, it comes as a small, still voice in the quiet of our mind. In order to hear, we need to tune out the background chatter, tame the cluttered thoughts of the circus within our mind, and then turn our attention – and the fullness of our affection – toward Jesus.

The whole point of this message is not just listening – but listening so as to hear God's voice for one purpose: to understand the message. Keep the idea of "understand" at the forefront of your mind as you read – because this is what the Lord wants to do throughout this message, and it will guide you toward the destination that God has in mind for you. The Lord wants us to *'akouo' – hear and understand.*

The three-fold <u>reasons</u> why the Lord wants us to hear His voice:

1. To believe (the truth)
2. To understand (His plan for our life, what we are to do, and to know why)
3. To obey (the words of Christ)

The five-fold <u>results</u> why He wants us to hear His voice:

1. Be sanctified (no longer conformed to this world, but conformed to Christ)
2. Be in Communion (to live in oneness and newness with Him every day)
3. Do His will (obey, endure, persevere, have dominion, occupy, advance)
4. Receive a commission (to proclaim and testify as faithful witnesses)
5. Worship (to love Him as He desires to be worshipped and adored)

Can You Hear God's Voice?

A: Absolutely! Because God created everyone with the ability to communicate with Him.

How do I know this is the truth?

A: Because this truth is confirmed in scripture, and God has already been speaking to you, and furthermore... because His message has already gone out to everyone (Rom. 10:18); however, you might not have known it was Him.

All species of animals communicate with one another, and every species (dogs, squirrels, whales, birds) have their own language – even within each species, and since you are a spiritual being having a human experience, therefore... your primary language is spiritual and your secondary (natural) language is earthly. In order to hear God's voice, you need to reactivate your spiritual ears – with a softened heart and sound mind. This is the hardest part of hearing – because if no one taught you about this spiritual language, then you must be taught a new language. Welcome to "How to hear God's voice – better."

Who Can Hear?

Listening to hear God's voice is not delegated by God to certain people with a special anointing like prophets or priests or pastors in order to hear and tell others His message; His voice is speaking to as many as are willing to hear – and understand – even to your children's children as far of as they may be. God speaks to everyone regardless of who they are – high church/low church or no church, sinners or saints, intelligent or stupid, rich or poor, ancient or modern, primitive or whatever... God speaks to all His children regardless of who they are – or where they are – or when they lived upon the earth.

> "For I know the thoughts that I think toward you, says the LORD, thoughts of peace and not of evil, to give you a future and a hope. [12] Then you will call

upon Me and go and pray to Me, and I will listen to you. [13] And you will seek Me and find Me, when you search for Me with all your heart" (Jer. 29:11-13).

The LORD said: "I know the thoughts (plans; NIV) that I have for you" – and if He has thoughts and plans '*machashabah*-4284' "purpose, plan, thought, intention,"[1] then He wants to tell you about those plans. If you want to hear "your" message, then you must go to the Source!

God wants us to know Him, know His thoughts and His ways. This is not a divine mystery but an open invitation – to know and understand His character and to walk in His ways.

"How precious also are Your thoughts to me, O God! How great is the sum of them! [18] If I should count them, they would be more in number than the sand; when I awake, I am still with You" (Psa. 139:17, 18).

God loves us beyond our ability to comprehend it! His thoughts toward us are good – always – and His thoughts for us and our well being are exceedingly numerous. And God wants to tell us all about His thoughts toward us… if only we would get still… and hear His small still voice.

Everyone can hear God's voice – if you want to hear it. The scriptures also document where this conversation takes place.

"And he *thought* within himself, saying, 'What shall I do, since I have no room to store my crops? [19] And I will say to my soul, "Soul, you have many goods laid up for many years"'" (Luke 12:17, 19).

This is a very interesting message Jesus is teaching us. The word

---

[1] Strong's Concordance.

"*thought*" is '*dialogizomai*-1260' (*dialogos*: literally – through words; English-dialogue) and means: "to reckon thoroughly, to deliberate (by reflection or discussion)" and is translated "reason, think, dispute, consider"[2] oftentimes to calculate the purpose or reason before taking action. Thoughts enable us to deliberate "our" purpose and actions – through words, but with whom are we deliberating? With "whom" are we speaking to and reasoning within our mind? So I ask: do you talk to yourself? And if yes (because everybody does), then how do you talk to yourself? Don't you need at least two thought generators in order to have a conversation? A: yes.

Your soul is composed of two elements: mind and heart. When they dialogue, the mind assembles information and then plants these thoughts and ideas into the heart to sift through facts and discern the matter to arrive at a joint decision. The mind and heart were designed by God to operate in oneness to perceive a matter; this oneness represents the conscience of a person in action. They are dialoging with one another to perceive the matter and see if it is aligned with the thing being perceived.

> "I call to remembrance my song in the night; I meditate within my heart, and my spirit makes diligent search" (Psa. 77:6).

"The thinker (the mind) – in union with the knower (the heart) – best describes: the conscience (*suneidesis*-4893) meaning: co-perception; with perfect knowing.[3] The thinker and the knower seek truth to understand perfectly what God planned for us. Thus, the moral consciousness of man is the result his conscience operating in co-perception (mind with heart) oneness of his soul."[4]

God designed us to operate in co-perception oneness (the conscience) to discern truth – and implement it. If one of these has

---

[2] Strong's Concordance; excerpt copied from "Commission" section titled: "Power In Operation" p. 88.
[3] Strong's Concordance.
[4] Excerpt copied from "Gateways" section titled "Gateways and Gatekeepers."

been deceived, corrupted by lies or is operating in error, a schism resulting in a seared conscience occurs whereby these persons are more likely to adopt thought patterns and lifestyles that are in opposition to God's truth. Rebellion is the result.

"Your thinker put understanding in your knower (either consciously or subconsciously), then your knower helps your thinker choose wisely. Our conscious *with* co-perception of mind and heart oneness is the balance we need in order to make good moral decisions, to understand the message of truth, to operate with justice and mercy toward one another, and to walk humbly before God with an upright heart. (Micah 6:8)"[5]

Why Do We Want To Hear?

If you want to know God's thoughts regarding His plans for you, then you are at the threshold of hearing His voice. Listening to hear – will happen if you truly want to hear – because God created us with an ability to hear His plans for us, so that – when we listen intently for the small still Voice… His Voice is the One we hear.

We need to allow the Lord's thoughts to invade our reality. When we allow His thoughts to invade our silent reality – a reality that is not in competition against Him with a multitude of many voices and competing sounds, then "You will know His thoughts toward you." At this point, most people are asking: "***So, what does God's voice sound like?***" God's voice is not a sound… it is a spontaneous thought that enters into your mind that you were not thinking moments before.

Be Still and Know This

What do you think the first step is to hearing God's voice? When this question is put to a person or before a group of people, the answer that quickly comes to mind is this,

---

[5] Excerpt copied from "Commission" section titled "Minds Decide, Hearts Establish."

"Be still and know that I am God" (Psalm. 46:10).

Just as God is talking to us all the time with guiding thoughts, there are moments when He is speaking directly to us – with directive words. And we are the same way. We may be talking to God in one manner or another, but when we turn our thoughts toward Him with the fullness of our attention and affection, this, then, is when the Lord hears – and answers us – and the Divine Response enables us to hear His voice.

When we hear His voice, our lives become irrevocably changed, never again to rebel against the sound of Love left ringing in our heart. "You are My beloved" reverberates over and over within our consciousness, as soothing waves of truth washing upon the shore of our battered soul. Listening is important, but hearing produces life-giving liberty, freedom, joy and peace!

There are many words in our prayers, and we often fill the quiet void of prayer with a multitude of loquacious thoughts, but the Lord's desire for us is to just sit still, be quiet, and put all our thoughts away so that He can talk words of life to us. We must be still and listen because God wants to have a word with us, and the divine relationship is dependent upon it!

He knows our thoughts from far off and He already knows what we need – and God is in control – so put aside the prayer lists and the multitude of many words to simply do one thing: sit still and listen attentively. The Lord wants us to crawl up onto His "heavenly Father" lap like a little child to just sit there and let Him hold us – in Divine communion with Him. When we become still, then we know that He is God... and we come to know Him as *our* Abba Father.

The Lord wants this more than anything: a conversation with us. Prayer is less about our many words and petitions; prayer is more about a personal relationship whereby we are listening for the sound of His voice. This requires two-way communication, not one-directional prayer, because our relationship with Him is dependent on it. How else are we going to know His ways or what

His character is like, or what He desires us to do? The Lord desires this because He wants to have and maintain a deep, abiding personal relationship with us.

Can you have a personal relationship with someone you cannot see, touch or hear? No. And so it is with God; He wants us to be able to experience Him in a personal way – and this way is often through listening and then hearing His voice. Ever since the beginning, there has been an open invitation to walk with Him in the garden of our heart, but we have erected doctrinal roadblocks along the path of faith and have overcomplicated the divine relationship.

God wants us to know Him, to know His thoughts and to walk in His ways.

Many Christians believe they have a personal relationship with Jesus, but there are oftentimes many unanswered questions, as well as many unanswered prayers, that may leave us wondering... am I praying correctly? Am I listening correctly? If He can hear our thoughts and prayers, then why doesn't He hear – and respond? Some of this confusion originates in our theological beliefs about what it means to have a personal relationship with the Divine. If you have never heard the Lord's voice in a personal, experiential manner, than how do you know that God loves you and cares for you – or that He even exists?

Jesus said, "**My sheep hear My voice, and I know them, and they follow Me**" (John 10:27).

This stands to reason, then, that if we consider ourselves Christians and followers of Christ, then we have heard His voice, right? At some level, yes, absolutely, and this is how we came to faith in Christ, being guided by the Holy Spirit, to come to Jesus and make a holy profession, but the divine relationship must continue past salvation's open invitation; the divine conversation must continue in order to strengthen us to be who we are supposed to be: His image bearers who are being conformed to His image and are, thereby, being transformed to live according to His example (likeness).

> "Do you have a personal relationship with Jesus – or do you have a theology that says you have a personal relationship with Jesus?" (Mark Virkler)

This is fundamentally important. I have known people who talk to the Lord as an everyday, natural, streaming flow of consciousness that acknowledges His presence within every breath; and I have seen gigantic spiritual tanks who can preach, teach, proclaim, operate in the gifts of the Spirit and heal the sick, but the hearing that comes like the faith of a small child just cannot be that simple … because, if prophets heard His audible voice, then that must be the *only* way to hear God. Hum. Do you want the God you want – or do you want the God who is? Let me say this ever so gently: God speaks to us to reveal Himself – which is often referred to as revelation. He can do this though the simplicity of His glory found in creation, talking donkeys, dreams and visions, written words, spoken words, the whisper of the wind, the wonder of stars in the heavens, an audible voice, a small still voice, fragrant aromas, or the tender touch of a child holding your hand. God is real – He can do whatever He wants and He can use an infinite number of ways to express Himself however He determines – but know this: He wants to invade our tangible reality with a conscious awareness of His nearness within us. He desires to have a conversation with us! If God can commission a star to tell three wise men where to go or divide a sea to lead a nation through a wilderness with a pillar of fire, why then, can't we accept the fact that He wants to talk to us as a small, still voice within us? It can't be that simple, can it? Yes, indeed! And it is!

A True Story

One day, I was teaching a class about hearing God's voice, and quite unexpectedly, I was confronted by the opinion of an individual whose theological and doctrinal premise stated the only way to hear God's voice was audible. How shockingly depressing! … as if God only speaks audibly, in one way or in one manner, so as to limit the infinite nature of God to elemental teachings that place God in a box. Then I wondered about how he would respond to those who talk to God regularly with the small still voice, or experience His wisdom through dreams and visions, or receive words of wisdom by reading the Bible, or have their conscious pricked when listening to a sermon preached specifically just for them. Not long after this, I was talking to a new acquaintance about hearing God's voice and she said her tradition does not accept dreams or visions; they were for the first century church age, somehow, completely bypassing Acts 2:39. I was, um, well, quite perplexed. With a grieved heart, I asked the Lord about it, knowing that a new great awakening is coming upon Christianity, the likes of which the institutional and indoctrinated church will likely disregard, and worse yet, profane and reject with outright contempt. How dare anyone teach the simplicity of hearing God's voice! Indeed, how dare we preach heretical insults to 2,000 years of tradition, and yet, here I was, wrestling with this reality from a class member and a neighbor who were thoroughly indoctrinated in a "God only expressed Himself through spiritual gifts in the first century church admin age." As I pondered these opinions, I asked the Lord for understanding about this situation, knowing that an even more potent age of glory, grace and power is on the foreseeable horizon, and then this streaming thought came to me: "we need a bigger boat."

God will always be bigger than our theology and our ability to understand of His thoughts and His ways; however, that is not the whole point, now, is it? Our belief or understanding about the truth does not have to be perfect, but our faith in the Perfect One must be true, genuine and authentic. It is not about having a right or wrong theology, it is about being willing to hear and obey in a right relationship with Him – and even being open to making mistakes. God is the One doing it – and He is doing it – in us, with us, to us, and through us!

What is going to happen is about to happen. It will be incredible, like a tremendous shaking that loses mountains from their foundations, like a tremendous blowing that unhinges leaves from trees, like the torrent of a rushing tsunami; it will be unlike anything the world has ever seen before, and the institutional church has no clue what is about to happen. It will be easier for this church to attack it – than change!

> "But why do you call Me 'Lord, Lord,' and not do the things which I say? [47] ***Whoever comes*** to Me, ***and hears*** My sayings ***and does*** them, I will show you whom he is like: [48] He is like a man building a house, who dug deep and laid the foundation on the rock. And when the flood arose, the stream beat vehemently against that house, and could not shake it, for it was founded on the rock. [49] But he who heard and did nothing is like a man who built a house on the earth without a foundation, against which the stream beat vehemently; and immediately it fell. And the ruin of that house was great" (Luke 6:46-49).

Keep It Simple

In an attempt to uncomplicate it, let me say this quite simply: don't make it complicated. Relax. Keep it simple. The truth of the Gospel is very simple: God is love and God loves us; He sent His Son to show us His love and He used words, workings and wonders to help us understand and, therefore, believe the proof of His message – and enter into faith. Jesus is Lord! Yet, man has an inherent, innate capacity to overcomplicate truth with religious theologies, dogmas and human-engineered doctrines, somehow believing we need to clarify the truth that God has already put in our heart. In short, we know the truth and we believe the truth, which we then proceed to put within boxes we call "understanding" and then we wonder why we don't understand God's truth when it becomes manifest outside our theological boundaries.

If you can define God or put His truth into a nice neat box, then I say this from experience: your box is too small. The Lord is expanding and changing my "God Box" every day with more understanding about who He is, what He is doing, and what He wants us to do, so, let's keep an open mind – and a soft heart – and we will not be disappointed, nor will be shaken, nor will we be left behind.

Well, if listening is so simple, then why doesn't everybody just hear Him and get on with world peace? Why not, indeed! That was the plan, and still is, but as you will see in the unfolding of truth, there are many things that we place between God and ourselves that either prevents us from hearing His voice, hinders our ability to discern His voice, or we choose to be the governor of our post-conversion, faith-walk journey. Once we are able to hear His voice and experience His presence in our lives, then we will have peace – we will experience His peace – and then we can share this peace with the entire world.

The Lord has a plan for us and we need to be able to hear His voice. Short and simple, this is the plan: listen, hear, understand, obey, have dominion, keep your eyes focused on Jesus only.

Before we can hear, we need to place ourselves in a receptive and reflective posture where we are actively listening to hear Him, because – hearing is different than listening. We are always listening because we have ears to listen for the sense of sound, but hearing is an active form of listening that is more attentive. Let's call it – active listening and attentive harkening; it requires a response, one way or the other. Listening and understanding are two components of one element: hearing. It demands a response.

In the above list regarding the Lord's plan for us, I would have put "obey His commands" as the second instruction, but some of us who are reading these words would immediately balk at the word 'obey,' as if God treats us like subservient puppets, so, let me put it to you like this: 'listen intelligently.' The Greek word for obey does not mean to respond in a subservient, submit-without-question, puppet, will-less, automaton-like manner. God gave us free will and you can decide on your own whether you want to listen, hear and do what He tells you – or not. The choice is yours. However, know this… the complexity of the human mind was designed by God so that – we can hear His voice. Think about that.

Terms

The Hebrew word for obey (8085) '*shama*' – means, "to listen intelligently;" and the Greek word for obey (5219) '*hupakouo*' – means "to listen attentively." The Jewish profession of faith, The Shema (a derivative of shama) simply means: hear – and obey. Obedience simply means: to listen intelligently – and do it. We are not puppets – we are listeners who hear His voice!

When we combine this contextual meaning of obey with *faith* (*pistis* – a firm persuasion, a conviction based upon hearing[6]), which is interpreted to mean – "being thoroughly persuaded and convinced," it begins to sound something like this:

Having been thoroughly persuaded and convinced by listening intelligently – obedience results according to faith through hearing.

Faith, in this instance, is not a thing: it is choice whereby the mind has made a firm decision, having been thoroughly persuaded and convinced, to understand and thoroughly believe what you heard – and thus, *faith is living according to what you believe is truth.* This is *pistis* faith in action. You don't have it; rather, it has you!

"For who, having heard, rebelled?" (Heb. 3:16)

When we hear the Lord's word spoken to us, it changes the way we think. Indeed, it must change us, or else we have only listened – without hearing to understand and obey. It must change us, or it is not believed on account of unbelief, and when it is not acted upon in faith, then the Lord considers this unbelief – as sin.

---

[6] Vine's Expository, word study on faith.

Consider this example: if a prophetic word was spoken over you, would you believe it? Some traditions do not even practice this, even though it is scripturally sound, so let me ask it differently… if someone told you it was going to rain today, even though the skies are sunny when you looked up, would you take an umbrella? Of course, you would. If someone told you that you were going to win the lottery today (hypothetically speaking), would you go out and immediately purchase a lottery ticket? Of course you would, but why, then, do we treat hearing God's voice any differently? How come we do not want to hear God's voice, even though they are all full of wonderful promises? Perhaps, it is because we really don't want to obey Him.

I confidently believe that, if you have ever heard His voice, you will never disobey Him again – ever! What God speaks is for our good and we can trust Him at His word (Rom. 8:28).

Some of you will find this next thought interesting: did Jesus ever tell us to obey Him? The winds and the seas obeyed Him (Matt. 8:27; Mark 4:41; Luke 8:25) and unclean spirits obeyed Him (Mark 1:27), and the Lord Jesus even told the disciples that "if you have faith," they could command a mulberry tree to be lifted up by its roots to be planted in the sea and it would obey them (Luke 17:6), *but* – Jesus never told us to obey Him.

If Jesus is your Lord, then you must obey Him within the context of your relationship with Him and His Lordship over you.

Jesus told us to listen with prepared hearts that are ready to hear, and then Jesus said, "If you love Me, you will *keep* My commandments" (John 14:15). The word "keep" is *'tereo'* (5083) meaning, "to watch, to guard (from loss or injury, properly, by keeping the eye upon)[7]. Jesus is telling us to safeguard His commandments and protect them from injury or loss by keeping an eye on them – as an act of love in faithful obedience to Him. So, how do we do this? We are motivated by our love for Jesus as

---

[7] Strong's Concordance.

faithful disciples – and our love is the bond of our covenant with Him.

Before we go any further, I just want to make sure that no one misinterprets my words to suggest that I am telling anyone not to obey the words of Jesus. Heaven forbid that anyone comes to such a conclusion, but such is life in a highly electrified dogmatic world! I am trying to teach the substance of faith, whereby hearing and obedience is one interconnected spiritual principle as it relates to hearing God's voice.

> "We ought to obey God rather than men" (Acts 5:29).

When you are actively listening to hear the Lord's voice, then you are living in a prepared state of readiness to hear His voice; you are living attentively; you have placed yourself, willingly, in a submissive posture to hear – and obey – the *rhema* (*utterance*) word of the Lord. We are all subservient to God regardless of whether you are doing it intentionally, through faith, or you are living in a state of rebellion. All humans are subservient, but not all have surrendered their will to Jesus; for until He becomes Lord of your life so that He alone is Lord of all, then you are just a human seeking a spiritual experience. The Lord Jesus is Master, Ruler, Sovereign, and King. If you have converted your self will and your total allegiance to Jesus as your Lord in the knowledge of the truth and you are living in obedience, then your life will joyfully conform to the will of God because you trust Him – unreservedly. You are all in; whatever God tells you to do – so let it be done – as much as it lies within you. We have all asked God "why" and have searched to comprehend the reasons why many things happen, but to the person who is all in, it doesn't matter. This is not living in blind trust, as in believing without basis of knowledge or understanding, but rather, this trust comes from having comprehended the truth, having been thoroughly persuaded and convinced – and these persons have been converted by this living truth to willingly walk in the Way of Christ. Jesus loves you and will care for you – always! This is the kind of love that you just can't irreverently ignore any more.

> "My sheep hear My voice, and I know them, and
> they follow Me" (John 10:27).

For many years, I considered this verse a metaphor that applies to doing the Lord's will, whereby believers are obedient compliant sheep who go to church on a regular basis, yet goats butt heads with God. I never took this scripture literally – until I began to listen. Perhaps the only thing that truly separates sheep from goats is their ability to hear and obey. If this is true, then our final determination after death may not be based upon what we believe, but rather, our faithful attentiveness to hearing God's voice – with obedience. Therefore, our eternal salvation is more dependent upon hearing His voice than following a multitude of doctrines and ordinances.

When He calls you by name, will you be able to hear? Will you be able to recognize the sound of His voice?

Many of us are wandering around planet earth – wondering why we have never heard the Lord's voice if He is talking to us all the time. God is everywhere, God is around us – and He is already within us, so why can't we hear Him? In our frustration, we give up, never knowing why some people can hear Him and we cannot. I also experienced this same frustration, so much, that I decided to go my own way. That, my friends, was a big mistake. God wants to have a personal relationship with all His children, so, what would you do if you were having a conversation with your child and they just walked away? And perhaps worse yet… they said, "whatever" and then walked away. Wouldn't you feel disrespected and disregarded? Of course you would – and so does our heavenly Father feel this rejection when we turn and walk away.

This thing I have learned: press in. Continue to seek Him diligently and earnestly. All these things I was doing, but I was still unable to hear His voice, so what was wrong? I learned that I was not approaching the throne of grace with honor, respect – and humility; I was coming to God as "an equal, not as someone on a lesser footing." I was not coming to Him in a subservient and reverent manner; I was still lord of my life and king of my kingdom. It wasn't until I completely surrendered my will, my life, my hopes and dreams, my agenda, and my kingdom – that I was finally able to hear His voice.

The Process of Hearing and Believing

How can we listen intelligently if we have *never* been thoroughly persuaded and convinced that God is sovereign and He governs the heavens and the earth? Sadly, we cannot. We need to get to the place where we submit to the Lord as the Governor of our soul whereby... "It is no longer I who live, but Christ who lives in me" (Gal. 2:20). We need to get to the place of total, complete surrender where God is in control – and you completely understand this heavenly truth. Yes, I got 2-20'd and my life has never been the same since (wonderfully awesome, that is).

On September 2012, a sister in Christ spoke two groups of thought to me; the first one you've read before: "You forgot who you are" became the impetus for my initial book: Regenesis (2014). The second group of words was essentially, "Sit down, shut up and get out of the way." Those were not the exact words she said to me, but that is how I remember them. It took me an entire year to learn the principle of "let go, let God, trust Him, He's got this – and – get (self) out of the way."

A year later, after I had been unemployed 26 of the previous 36 months, with no resources and heavily in debt, and credit cards were maxed, I could no longer afford to pay the mortgage or any other bills, yet this is when the Lord told me to start writing. He took me to a place where it was illogical for me to start writing because I had no financial resources and no foreseeable provision. He called me at a time when I did not have a job title, profession, position or alphabets after my name; I was just a gardener.

Then, on September 27, 2013, the Lord gave me understanding – and then these words, "You are My writer... now write." And then a few days later, a very clear Voice in my mind spoke three little words: "Wait for it." Even though I continued to submit resumes and received calls for interviews, employment doors never opened... not even a crack. After five months of this, I made a firm decision to stop applying for jobs and to trust completely, unreservedly and without preconceived ideas regarding how God was going to accomplish this work that He clearly called me to do. How could I, after hearing His voice, continue to doubt by applying for jobs and sending more resumes? Either I must live according to the truth I write, or else I have judged myself a hypocrite. I shared some of this story with my family – and you can all figure out what happened next. "How will you live? What will you eat? How will you.... (fill in the blank)." It was utterly ridiculous and preposterous that a person can live like that. No one ever said it, but I could read it in their eyes: "that's not the God I know... He would never do that or say that." Well, they were right about one part – that is not the God they know.

There is a dramatic difference between listening and hearing, just as there is a difference between looking and seeing. In both cases, the looker and listener is a seeker – as one who is in search of something, but when the seeker finally sees or hears, then they are no longer a seeker – now they are a finder. "Seek the Lord while He may be found" (Isa. 55:6). They now possess what they have diligently sought after. So, what should happen to such a one as this? Would you expect they will take this treasure of great value and pearl of great price and then – do nothing with it? Or even worse, hide it in a field or place it under a bushel basket? Anathema! Once you have found the truth, a genuine seeker will transition to a finder for just such a moment in time – and then they become a proclaimer!

Spiritual truth is exciting and life giving; it must be shared. Your wineskin will burst at the seams from the inexpressible joy of the good news that you have received (which is why God gives converts a new wineskin). The words may not come out clear and succinct at first, but the truth of the message is this: conversion. This person's life has just been changed – eternally! And they have to, are even compelled to, share the good news. The truth abiding within such a person will manifest an active change in their lifestyle (in contrast to the passive participant and spectator lifestyle). They have been transformed; now, they are a new creation... and the old man has passed away. Behold, a new person is now abiding in that earthen vessel (2 Cor. 5:17).

Truth is contagious – and it must be shared! You cannot help but not do it; such a one is compelled to share! Yes, even proclaim it from the rooftops!

> "But be doers of the word, and not hearers only, deceiving yourselves" (James 1:22).

The message is this: God wants to speak to you and me. God loves you so much that He wants to have a personal relationship with you and He wants to communicate with you and share divine truth with you – even revelation – *if* you are willing to hear. The divine relationship requires divine conversation – and one-way prayers don't count.

> "Today, if you will hear His voice, do not harden your hearts as in the rebellion" (Heb. 3:15).

How To Listen

There are many good teachings about how to hear God's voice and more are being written every day. Mark Virkler's teaching, "Four Keys" to hearing God's voice is also an excellent place to begin. I did not know about these teachings until I was already listening. I will share some thoughts and experiences of mine, but let me make just one point: God speaks to one person and then to another according to who they are. We are all different, so it is safe to assume that God will speak to each of us differently, individually, and yes, intimately. We may learn the spiritual principles of listening and how to hear God's voice and pick up some ideas and techniques, but it all comes down to one question: do you want to hear? I mean, do you really, really, truly want to hear God's voice? Be honest... are you willing to do whatever it takes to hear His voice? Would you be willing to surrender everything to hear

His voice? Would you be willing to surrender your life for a year in order to hear His voice? Are you coming to God to satisfy your agenda or do you desire to hear His voice – whatever the cost may be? It may be that ... all it costs is all you've got.

I can promise you one thing: when you hear His voice, your life will be dramatically changed, transformed and revolutionized. His voice is so awesome and amazing that you will never want to go back to your old life and live according those pitiful, meagerly, fleshly ways.

Are you willing to pay the price to hear – and are you determined to obey (listen intelligently) when the Lord commands you to do something? This is a serious question for a life-altering event which will happen; no maybes... it will happen! God desires it to happen! He wants us to hear, so, when you hear, the operative question is – will you obey?

You must remove the roadblock of disobedience in your mind that prevents you from hearing.

Before you can hear, you need to prepare your heart. If, for example, you were invited to visit the President of the United States or any other country, would you show up in sweatpants, t-shirt and uncombed hair? Neither would I – out of respect for the office – so don't come into God's presence and expect to receive a pearl of great price if you are ambivalent or insincere in your heart's motivations. Be respectful – be reverent. Do not doubt; believe!

If you have not totally surrendered your will to the Lord, or if you still consider yourself the master of your soul, or if you are only seeking "advice" from God regarding how you should live your life, or if you are just shopping for an opinion but *may* take His word "under advisement," then don't expect to receive or hear anything from the Lord. Such a person is double-minded, as one who is seeking truth from God yet remains entrenched in their own preconceived beliefs. You cannot stand in between two ways with

God on the matter of hearing His voice. Either you are all in or you are all out. Don't get me wrong… the Lord will never abandon you or forsake you, but if we come to Him seeking a blessing from Him rather than seeking Him, then the relationship that this person seeks with God is one-sided and self-serving. Do you desire God – or do you desire His things? God is only interested in building His kingdom, not yours!

Before we can enter into the good things that God has prepared in advance for us, we need to die to the flesh and all its' earthly desires. We are spiritual beings having a human experience, but it didn't take long in order for us to turn the spiritual paradigm upside down in order for us to focus all our energies on living for the flesh. There are multitudes that will read this and have no clue regarding what I am saying, so read "Regenesis" to learn *who* you really are – from God's perspective.

We cannot approach God with earthly ears in the hope of hearing spiritual words. We need to listen to God with our spirit-man, "For that which is spirit, spirit is" (John 3:6). Hearing from God is not an academic, intellectual or emotional exercise; it is a spiritual discipline. This is not something that you do over and over hoping to get it right, which is called practice and exercise. God told us precisely what we need to do in order to hear from Him: surrender all and declare Jesus Lord of all. As Jesus said: "My sheep hear My voice."

Many of us have tried to take shortcuts when it comes to hearing God's voice, but I had to find out the hard way the futility of that approach. There was only one way for me to hear His voice: I had to render myself dead. I had to present myself as a living sacrifice; I needed to be crucified with Christ; I had to put to death the desires of the flesh, the cares of this world as well as the deeds of the flesh, because the flesh wages war against the things of the spirit. Hearing God's voice is a spiritual discipline, so make no provision for the flesh. I desperately wanted to hear… so my flesh had to die!

After many months of hearing God's voice, without benefit of any income or provision, still journaling 5-10 pages a day, I began to doubt that I was listening to the voice of God... and then I heard it, loud and clear in my mind, "Did you think I wouldn't take care of you?" Let me tell you... all worry, fear and anxiety left in an instant. That is the power of hearing God's word – in spirit and in truth; peace was restored in my soul. This journey of faith and trust would have been impossible had I not been able to hear His voice. So, let me ask you again... do you want to hear? Do you desire to hear His wonderful beautiful voice above anything else?

Hearing requires us to be still, listen, wait, hear with understanding, believe – and then – take a step of faith

If you want to hear... then you will hear!

Hear Him!

The last two words from God that were spoken from heaven are the first words concerning Christ: "This is My beloved Son. Hear Him!" (Matt. 17:5; Mark 9:7; Luke 9:35).

We must all take a moment to pause and deeply consider these words: "Hear Him!" Don't just read your Bible and listen to Sunday sermons; listen attentively, listen intelligently. Listen, hear His voice – and obey. Once you have heard the sound of His voice, you will never want to return to Egypt. And, so it was with the nation Israel... God wanted to speak to them and have a personal relationship with them, but they did not want to listen. They preferred Egypt; they appointed Moses as the listener to hear on behalf of everyone. This was not God's plan, but this was their choice – and it was a bad choice. Since they didn't want to hear the *rhema* word of God's voice, He gave them over to the written word, which came as a Law with a command: "Cursed is anyone who does not confirm all the words of this law" (Deut. 27:26). If you cannot say Amen, then say ouch!

My Journey To Hear

My journey to hear God's voice was quite typical as with most believers. I would read the Bible and then scripture would leap off the page and become a living word to me. So, step one, read the Bible.

The Holy Spirit was on me and in me at this point, by faith, but as of yet I had not received the Baptism of the Holy Spirit, which is like wearing glasses without the correct prescription lenses. I was able to see the truth more clearly (after the baptism) – and this is when the Spirit's sanctification process began to change the way I think and perceive God's kingdom truth. But before I got the baptism (of the Holy Spirit), the Lord had to remove some grievous areas of sin in my life. If there are active areas of sin in your life, then God is already speaking to you through the Holy Spirit, who convicts the world of sin – to depart from sin. Even though you have been converted, if you have yet to be convicted, then you are not listening. Sin creates a wall of separation between you and God, and hinders your spiritual ability to hear God's voice. God is always talking and we are always listening, but the issue at hand is the ability to hear.

As a young Christian, I remember praying this prayer often, "If you make your will perfectly clear to me, then I will never disobey You." I still pray that prayer. When we hear, then we must obey, or else the conversation stops. Have you made this concrete determination in your own spiritual life?

Most of the messages I've heard from the Lord were what I call impressions: I believe the Lord is saying this – or – I think I hear the Lord saying that. I was an immature Christian… what can I say. Then I began to get chapter and verse scripture references in my mind as the result of prayer, so, I would look them up and, sure enough, the answer was written down; I just needed the Holy Spirit to guide me. We _must_ be guided and directed by the Holy Spirit. Period!

Then came the "I got this" period, when I thought I knew what God wanted, so I just did it. This wasn't confidence in the Lord, it was self-serving pride and arrogance. The next time you say "I got this" to God – and then He tells you to "go for it," this is when a loving Father is teaching His child not to run ahead or go our own way. Chastisement happens... at the end of a long leash. Check your spirit and check these plans in the company of good counsel.

If you cannot hear clearly, then perhaps other saints in your vicinity will get a word from the Lord. (Please understand – we are not to run to other humans, pastors or clergy every time we need a word from the Lord. God wants us to talk to Him, so ask Him first, but if we cannot hear, then He instituted plan "B" i.e. wise counsel. Plan A is to listen to what the Spirit is telling you and do it. Plan B is to get confirmation from others.) What may seem like a perfect plan to us – often is, but this plan may be all about building *our* kingdom. God will let us have our way for a season – and then shipwreck happens. We are not on this earth to satisfy our agenda or the agendas of our various denominations. We are here to serve the Lord and to establish the kingdom of heaven on earth with the atmosphere of grace. If it smells more like flesh than grace, then shift the atmosphere.

> "For God may speak in one way, or in another, yet man does not perceive it" (Job 33:14).

After many years of walking my own path, shipwreck happened; I found myself subsisting day by day during a dark season of chaos and confusion in my life until I grew desperate to hear His voice. One day, I opened a daily devotional – Jesus Calling (by Sarah Young) – and then the process of hearing and believing began *again*. Sarah is a listener who writes what she hears Jesus is saying to her. It is poignantly obvious to even casual readers just how much Jesus loves us – and how much He wants us to hear His voice. It only takes a couple minutes to read each day, and as I meditated on the truth found on these pages, it seemed "coincidental" that many of those daily devotions were written specifically for me – really... just for me! This is how the Holy

Spirit works, as He guides us to the truth, day by day, truth by truth… until an awakening in our spirit happens.

Eventually, about a year later, the Lord brought me to a place where I had to give up and completely surrender, and the prayer of my heart was the prayer of Moses:

> "Now therefore, I pray, if I have found grace in Your sight, show me now Your way, that I may know You and that I may find grace in Your sight" (Ex. 31:13).

Show Me Your Way…

This is when the Lord really began to speak to me because I (my ego aka self) was no longer the focus; I was interested only in knowing Jesus more and more. I wanted to truly know God and completely comprehend God's ways – and therefore, Jesus became my focus for living!

I made the decision to be "all in" and I wanted to walk in His way. As I focused more attention on Jesus, I spent more time just listening is quiet, stillness and peace. During this time, while I was resting in His presence, the Spirit was washing over my mind with thoughts filled with understanding and grace. I was being transformed by the renewing of my mind and my soul was being refreshed. One day, while meditating on the Word, the Spirit had me look up a scripture:

> "Be still and know that I am God" (Psalm. 46:10).

The word "still" is '*raphah*' (7503) and means – "to be slacken; be feeble, weak, slack, faint."[8] Used within the context of the scripture above, it has an inherent meaning to draw toward (God) and forsake (self). As I waited in the Spirit and listened more intently, I began to notice how I had become motionless, soundless and selfless, such that the sound of my breathing had become

---

[8] Strong's Concordance.

noticeably loud. During these times, I would remain still for long periods of time, once as long as three hours without flinching, whereby this created a new terminology for me to describe stillness and slacken… when you become so unmoved that you resemble a cooked noodle that is cast upon the floor; where it lands is how it remains… motionless in His Presence.

Another aspect of stillness is… to know God. In fact, it is the main purpose of listening in stillness! Be still… and know that I am God. Be still… "and then you will know that I am God because I will speak with you." The Lord wants to speak to us and He will speak to us when our heart's attention and affection is focused entirely on Him.

Now, whenever I am troubled or perplexed by anything, I quickly return to '*raphah*' stillness to hear His voice. Forsaking all busyness with self-purposed plans, schedules and agendas is one of our highest callings in Christ – so that we may focus our eyes upon Him, hear His voice and enter into His rest. As my sister in Christ said to me… "Sit down, shut up and get out of the way." We need to let go of everything, cease all striving, and then get "self" out of "the way" in order to enter into His fullness and Presence wherein everything becomes ordered according to His purposes and plans under heaven – and in our lives.

Stillness, in quiet repose and meditation, is how I focus on Christ each morning as I am waking up – where Divine realignment of my will is surrendered in faithful obedience unto Him. My day does not begin with the alarm clock – it begins in newness by focusing on Jesus my Lord.

It has been out of this understanding that I have been writing, so let me recap the steps I go through in order to hear God's voice.

Hearing Basics

1. You must be birthed by the Spirit and born anew according to the Spirit of life in Christ Jesus (John 3:3; Rom. 8:1) in order to understand how the kingdom of God operates, but this cannot happen unless the old man is reckoned dead. You cannot be standing in between two ways. We are born anew by the Spirit to build God's kingdom, not our own.
2. Repent of any sin. If there is sin in your life and you are living life according to the flesh that leads to sin, then there will be a dividing wall of separation between you and God that will hinder your ability to hear. So, clean out every room of your house first, including that secret closet. Confess all sin in your life – and repent. If sin separates us from God, then it will also hinder us from hearing His voice.
3. Walk in the Spirit. It is always a good idea to experience the Holy Spirit baptism before you proceed because your walk with Jesus is dramatically supercharged by the Spirit in order to live according to the manner in which we were created, as image bearers with ears to hear, but since many denominations do not encourage this expression, and some denominations even teach what is contrary to scripture that this baptism doesn't exist (even so, seek it anyway), but if it hasn't happened to you thus far, this will not prevent you from hearing His voice. He got you this far, hasn't He?
4. The enemy, also, has access to your mind, especially during very tumultuous and stressful periods of trial and tribulation, and also during times when you are pressing in to God, so pray a hedge of protection around yourself so the enemy cannot get in (Job 1:10; 3:23) and put a hedge around the enemy to keep them bound (Hosea 2:6). In the delegated authority that Jesus has given you, bind the deceiver "in Jesus' name." Satan is only allowed to speak into your mind *if* you have given him permission to speak there. Remember this truth: when we believe the lie, we empower the liar, so remove all falsehood and unbelief. Resist the devil – and he must flee from you! (James 4:7)

When we bind (silence) the deceiver, then this is one less voice we will hear.
5. Get quiet and remove all the background noise in your mind. If you have a restless mind that won't stop processing endless thoughts, then I will offer some tips (below). This was my main problem, what I call "restless mind syndrome." We need to be quiet – and still our thoughts. We need to become very still in order to silence the other voice in our mind – me, my and mine – which is the ego voice of self.
6. Once you are perfectly quiet, then pray in the Spirit with your spirit. You do not need to verbalize words or make any sounds because God can hear our thoughts (Gen. 18:12-13) and knows the intents of our heart (1 Chron. 28:9; Luke 5:22). Some of us have been errantly taught that we must speak aloud when we pray, as if God only hears spoken words, but this seems to be just another false teaching from the enemy to make noise when we should be quiet in the meditations of our heart. Simply talk to God as you would a friend because God is not impressed with long-winded, pious sounding prayers. I often pray for just a few moments, and then I start listening. If your thoughts spring up, then get quiet again. God does not compete with background chatter or multi-tasking thoughts. "Be still… and know that I am God" (Psa. 46:10). Once you are perfectly still, by faith – you are abiding in His presence – and God will speak to you.
7. A thought, idea, word or song will come to your mind. You know in your heart that you did not think this, nor did you invent it or use human effort to create it, and the enemy did not utter it because they have been silenced; therefore, the Holy Spirit spoke it into your mind. Hooray! You just heard God's voice. This was a spontaneous "utterance" from the Lord that is often followed by joy and much peace. Now, I can answer one of the earlier questions, "What does God's voice sound like?" It comes, not as a sound, but as a *spontaneous thought* deep within you.

8. Now, tune to flow. The Lord has been waiting for this moment since the beginning. He desires to have a conversation with you and to fellowship with you. He desires a personal relationship with all His children – so continue to be still and listen. I have often spent hours like this. Even when the Lord is silent, I know that I am in His presence and my soul and spirit are receiving spiritual healing, nourishment and blessing.
9. This next part is very important; write down what you hear. Journaling is very important, so when the Lord has given you a word, write it down. The enemy wants to attack you with thoughts of doubt and unbelief, so put out those fiery darts and arrows with the written word. Do not empower the enemy; extinguish all fear, lies, doubt and unbelief with truth.

Once you have begun to hear the voice of God, unusual things will begin to happen in your life that are born in the spiritual realm, so be attentive to discerning God voice – as well as the deceptive lies of the enemy. If a spontaneous thought comes to you, but it is clearly not from the Lord, like sexual perversion or negative thoughts about people, this is because there are demons in the world that will come to you as lying spirits with demonic thoughts. Do not entertain these thoughts, reject them outright, take them captive and send them back to the pit where they belong – in Jesus' name. And one more thing, forgive yourself quickly. Brush this memory off just as quickly as it came because it wasn't yours, so don't own it – and don't beat yourself up for having it. This was an attack by the enemy. Disregard the enemy! Push them aside! Stay focused on Jesus – and go back to listening.

It may surprise you to know that all spiritual language is within the realm of thought. Both kingdoms – of light and darkness – are able to speak into your mind and influence you either for good or for evil. Sitting at "the table of your mind" are three entities: you, God, and Satan. Your heart and spirit are also in attendance, as they are under the governance of your soul, but I want to key in on the three entities at this table. Dialogue – through words – is happening all the time because all three have a right to be there, but you determine who speaks and communicates at the table of your mind.

> "For as we have many members in one body, but all the members do not have the same function" (Rom. 12:4).

How do we know if our mind is susceptible to demonic influence? The Apostle Paul told us so.

> "I find then a law, that evil is present with me, the one who wills to do good" (Rom. 7:21).

> "But I see another law in my members, warring against the law of my mind, and bringing me into captivity to the law of sin which is in my members" (Rom. 7:23)

If you want to hear God's voice better, then you have to silence the other two voices.

Satan can speak to anyone, and indeed he does, but if he is commanded to keep silent and not given permission to speak, then that is one less voice at the table. This is mission critical if you have purposed in your heart and mind to be a disciple for Jesus:

You must silence the enemy!

It is imperative to understand this point: all spiritual language is within the realm of thought! Some of it may be manifested as utterances and spoken words, but all spiritual language originates as expressions and thoughts. The expression precedes the manifestation.

How do we silence the enemy?

I have a very simple process of silencing the enemy when I want to hear God's voice on very important matters, which I use prior to prayer, and especially before intercessory prayer!

1. The enemy can hear all our words and they can see our actions, so if you have a private personal matter that you are lifting up in prayer, then keep your prayers silent. God hears all our thoughts because He dwells in everyone, so it is not necessary to pray audibly; the divine conversation (dialogue – with words) between me and the Lord is always by silent thought language, so I encourage you to do likewise – in your mind. In this manner, the enemy cannot influence my prayers with evil ideas because they have no clue what I am praying about – yet when the Lord responds to my specific prayer request, it is with great confidence that I have heard the delightful *rhema* of my Lord.
2. Pray a protective covering over yourself. I begin prayer this way: "Jesus, you are my Lord and protector, hide me under the shadow of your wing, and protect me under the shield of faith." This simple prayer is two-fold: 1) once you are hidden in Christ, the enemy is unaware of your location and you can proceed with spiritual warfare without them knowing who you are or (more importantly) where you are. You will come under enemy attack, to be certain, so don't leave yourself vulnerable to attack by making yourself an open target, and 2) the shield of faith will protect you from the arrows of the enemy. Many people suffering from headaches and physical anomalies during periods of intense prayer and ministry are literally being attacked by weapons from the enemy.
3. Saints, if you pray to Jesus the same way every day, then understand this: the enemy knows what you are going to do even before you start. And if you have verbalized your thoughts or prayers, then they have a good idea what you will be praying for (even in silence – days or weeks from now) whereby they may influence your mind with preemptive thoughts which you may interpret as words from the Lord. This has happened to me a couple times, so I caution you to keep private spiritual matters between you and the Lord – silent. If you are going to pray about a matter with another saint, which I strongly encourage you

do, then begin any and every prayer session (small or large) with this simple prayer:

"In the authority the Lord Jesus has given to me, I take authority over (name them) – powers, principalities, strongholds, and every wicked and unclean demon, devil and spirit that is raised up against Jesus Christ and the knowledge of God, and I command you all to go back to the pit where you belong – in the name of Jesus."

Then I pray: "And I bind you there in silence – in the name of Jesus."

And then I pray: "Lord, I pray a hedge of protection around me and this place to prevent the enemy from entering in. In the authority you have given me, I cast them from this place and I bind them in their place, and I bind them in silence, and I place a hedge of protection around me (or church) to keep them (and other spirits) from entering."

Once you have bound the enemy, as that which we were taught by the Lord, "Whatever you bind or loose on earth is bound or loosed in heaven," the second part of this authority is the fun part: start loosing things from heaven onto earth. Worship and praise are audible forms of prayer that demons and wicked spirit cannot tolerate (it drives them crazy). Stop praying for new houses and new cars and worldly things; seek first the kingdom of God and pray for the New Earth where you will be able to enjoy (truly enjoy) true riches where thieves cannot steal (because they will all be in hell) and what moths and rust cannot destroy."[9]

Don't think of these prayers as a magic formula or incantation that works… because the power to rebuke the enemy does not happen by saying certain words – but by believing you have authority with

---

[9] Excerpt from "Commission."

power to speak against the enemy – and command them to flee. Words of truth (believed and acted upon) are the weapon of choice against your demonic enemy.

By silencing the enemy, that is one less voice we hear, but the voice of our soul must also be silenced by stillness so that we may meditate upon the Lord. For many of us, it is very difficult to become still and quiet, but you must discipline your mind, spirit and body to "be still" and remain quiet. I still struggle with a restless mind that will not stop thinking, so if you struggle in this area as well, then I invite you to keep reading to learn many steps to govern your thinking.

Saints, the enemy is at war with us and we must oppose the enemy with prayer; we fight this battle on our knees. If you are an intercessor, you will come under intense enemy attack, but do not let the enemy bludgeon you with assault upon assault. Silence the enemy and command them to be silent, but – first – hide yourself before doing so "under the shelter of His wing." Many intercessors are not standing upon the wall because some have (literally) born the pain and within their bodies felt the very same physical ailments, emotional wounding, mental confusion, fear, anger and depression of those for whom they are praying wherein the enemy simply redirected those attacks against them. Intercessors: you are valuable, so you are more vulnerable to attack, so cover yourselves in prayer… and get back up on the wall.

Three Simple Steps To Hearing

Here are my three simple steps to hearing God's voice anywhere, at any moment:

1. <u>Silence the enemy</u>. The mind is the battleground of thoughts (yours, God's and the enemy), so ask the Lord to hide you from the enemy under the shadow of His wing (they can't attack what they cannot find (Psa. 17:8, 9), pray a hedge of protection around yourself (Job 1:10; 3:23), then bind the enemy in silence with a hedge of thorns around

them (Hos. 2:6), put on the helmet of salvation (Eph. 6:14-18) and then pray the shield of faith over you. Take authority over the enemy with the authority that Jesus has given to all His followers *who abide in His presence* (Luke 10:17, 18), and in this manner, one less voice will come into your head. The name of Jesus is mighty for pulling down strongholds, scattering the enemy, and silencing the enemy. Believe that whatever you hear – will be His voice – and do not doubt.

2. <u>Silence yourself</u>. Clear your mind and your heart. Silence your thoughts and imaginations. We all have many thoughts and memories, presumptuous thoughts, preconceived ideas and vivid imaginations. Take ***all*** thoughts captive to the obedience of Christ. If any thought of past sin comes to mind, then ask for forgiveness and move on. Unforgiveness is one of the main obstacles preventing us from hearing His voice, so clear your heart and do not give the enemy a foothold. Declare your obedience to His sovereignty of thought in your mind and heart – and then – stop thinking. Let your mind be open to an infinite reality without sound or distraction. Tell your soul and spirit to be silent if they continue to make distractions (tell your soul to wait in silence – Psa. 62:1; 130:5; and command your spirit to be still – Isa. 26:9; 1 Cor. 6:20; Eph. 4:23).

3. <u>Be still</u> – "and know God is." Wait, not with a passive interest to *know* Him, but wait with expectant desire to *understand* Him as the great I AM. Wait for it. God is there, so be still and get to know I AM – because He really wants you to know Him, and to be known by Him, so trust and believe that He will speak to you. Above all else, seek His face and fix your eyes upon Jesus (Heb. 12:2). Focus on Jesus! Let His thoughts come to you and allow (permit) His way (of the Spirit) to flow through you. When you hear it, then journal it to make sure it is consistent (compatible) with scripture, ***but do not doubt!***

Let the Lord's thoughts invade your reality. When we allow His thoughts to enter into our silent reality – a reality that is not in competition against Him (drowning out His voice), then this scripture will be fulfilled in your hearing: "My thoughts are ~~not~~ your thoughts." God's thoughts become your thoughts as… God's thoughts in you. As you continue to hear His voice and do what He tells you to do, then you will be obediently fulfilling more scripture: "My ways are ~~not~~ your ways" as you begin to say and do things according to His ways, not your ways.

Akouo – hear and understand. Shema – hear and obey.
Keep it simple. God likes it that way.

The Lord dearly wants to have a conversation with us, and one of the first things He often tells the listener of His voice is … how much He loves you. If it takes you a week or an entire year like it took me, this singular moment causes time to stand still in His presence. He loves us so much and He wants to tell us – in person!

Sometimes, especially after I have been quiet for extended periods of time in one sitting, even a small sound will quicken me (jolt me to attention), but a loud noise, bang or hard knock at the door will cause me to leap out of my skin… causing my heart to race wildly for a few moments. (Note: if this happens and your heart is still racing, just cough really hard once or twice and your heartbeat will return to normal immediately.) So intense are these moments of listening that acorns landing on a metal shed roof can sound like gunfire, so don't be alarmed when this happens. And don't worry about these distractions; you left – God didn't. Just return to listening; this is what the Lord desires.

I had been hearing God's voice for about a year when, all of a sudden, something spiritually significant happened. I began waking up with a word, or a song, or a thought or an idea. I was not waking up to pray and communicate with God; I woke up and I was already praying and talking with God. It was as if my spirit was communicating with the Holy Spirit while I slept. This is now the most wonderful time of my day, when I am perfectly relaxed; I am not thinking about the day's agenda or anything else. I am peaceful, still, quiet – and listening. God had been waiting for this awakening of my spirit for 30 years of Christian faithfulness. He desires to speak to every one of us like this – and in this I am absolutely confident in the Lord – He desires to speak to you!

> "With my soul I have desired You *in the night*, yes, by my spirit within me I will *seek You early*; for when Your judgments are in the earth, the inhabitants of the world will learn righteousness" (Isa. 26:9).

My best time of the day is now in the early morning, but such was not always the case; I used to be a night owl. Your best time with the Lord will be whenever you are quiet, and when you are most attentive and alert, so seek Him during those times. This can happen anywhere at any time. God's phone number is 24/7/365. You can call and converse with Him anytime.

During these periods of time, when I was in stillness, I would get a word or a sentence or streaming thoughts one after another. I was always a ready writer, with pen and paper nearby (Psalm 45:1). And then it happened: I was seemingly baptized with His thoughts and I journaled about 150 pages in a couple weeks. It is nearly impossible to explain what happened during this time, but all I can say is "I began to get understanding." Prior to this, I would hear His voice and then write the words down, but these were not just a sentences – it seemed like I received entire book chapters all at once. Even today, now ten months later,[10] I am still writing out of that spiritual download of understanding by the Holy Spirit on September 27, 2013.

Let me encourage you in this. If God did this in my life, then He desires to do it in your life also. The manner may be different, but the means will be similar. We are the same, you and I… and God does not change. He is doing this to multitudes of people all around you – many of whom consider themselves "the hidden,"

---

[10] And now, even, many years later.

since we have been hidden in Christ Jesus for just such a time as this. We are listeners who hear – and obey – and the Lord is calling you to hear as well. Do not reject or disobey His invitation!

Later that week, as I was still glowing from the understanding that I had received, the Lord spoke three little words to me: "Wait for it." And I am still – patiently submitted – waiting for it today.

(Even now, as I have been guided to do so on 4/13/16, I have inserted this paragraph while waiting patiently for the Lord to tell me when to release this book – after finishing it 16 months ago. I don't want you to draw the wrong conclusion by this next comment, but if you can teach a dog to wait when every bone in their body is anxiously expecting to chase after the stick you threw and get it between their teeth, then that dog can be trained. And so it is with image bearers; when we hear the Lord' voice, it is important for us to understand the timing of the message given to us. Anticipating the reward comes with patient endurance – and the disciple of Jesus must always wait upon Him and be willing to wait for the moment when we no longer hear "Wait for it" but rather… "Attain it!" A word given in due season will produce much fruit. Disciples with a prophetic anointing become very much aware of this sense of timing *and release.* And while it is exceedingly important for us to hear, there will be times when we must also wait for the permission to release His word. The Apostle John waited and meditated 60 years before his gospel of Jesus or his other four books were written. Saints – we must not run ahead of the Messenger when we are given a message. Praise Him and give Him thanks for the message, then ask Him if today is the day to deliver the message. It's not about us – it's all about Jesus!)

Some months later, I began to share these words from the Lord with a friend, not knowing for sure if I had heard correctly. He encouraged me! These words were wonderful and life-giving, but, in all honesty, because they were so foreign to my doctrinal beliefs, I thought I was espousing heresy. A couple weeks later, I was sharing more testimony about the words I was hearing when another brother in Christ overheard the conversation and said to me, "Do you think you are the only one who thinks this way?"

Such is the case within Christianity today; there is a hidden remnant that is hearing God's voice, but they wonder if they are the only ones. Let me confidently assure you – you are not alone! There are words of wisdom and revelation happening all around us; people are seeing visions and having dreams; people are experiencing the presence of God in every denomination; miracles are occurring more frequently; signs and wonders are being manifest around us; people are seeing angels and are having supernatural experiences. Indeed, heaven is already thoroughly open and, now, even creation is anxiously expecting the sons of God to be revealed.

All this is happening, and will continue to happen, and will begin to accelerate quickly. Hear Him! God is calling you into more than just a spiritual relationship; He is calling you into divine service for His glory. How can you profess a personal relationship if you have never heard His voice? Can you claim a true friendship with anyone without having had a conversation with them? You are being activated for divine service, so get ready!

Several weeks after my 9/27/13 experience, in a manner that you might expect, I was praying, listening and then I heard the Lord's voice say: "Habakkuk 2." So, I looked it up and wrote it down. This scripture says, in part, "Wait for it." Several months later, I started taking a class about the "Four Keys" to hearing God's voice by Mark Virkler. When he put a scripture on the screen, I nearly flipped. Here it is:

> "I will stand my watch and set myself on the rampart, and watch to see what He will say to me, and what I will answer when I am corrected. [2] Then the LORD answered me and said: "Write the vision and make it plain on tablets, that he may run who reads it." (Hab. 2:1-2).

However, the next two verses of scripture were foremost in my consciousness because I was intimately aware of this scripture, having meditated on it often for several months:

> "For the vision is yet for an appointed time; but at the end it will speak, and it will not lie. Though it tarries, **wait for it**; because it will surely come, it will not tarry" (Hab. 2:3).

When you are listening for His voice, you will begin to experience supernatural (what I call, spirit-normal) events such as this, because now you are sensitive to the flow of the Spirit and you will experience what the Lord desires you to experience. You will hear the same scripture or a similar message over and over in multiple places, so pay attention to what the Spirit is saying to you at that time. This is not an experience to puff us up; these experiences are to encourage us to continue on the path that focuses our thoughts and our eyes upon Jesus only – whereby we give all glory to God!

We will begin to experience divine appointments, divine conversations, divine dreams and visions, and we will be given divine callings; *we are being activated* for divine service and we will be given divine '*dunamis*' miraculous power consistent with our divine nature (2 Pet. 1:3, 4). In this, God is glorified.

One morning, as I was waking up, I had a dream about a man in our church. We had chatted briefly about a year before and had crossed paths once since, so in that I knew who he was, I did not know him personally. The dream was vivid, and you could probably guess what happened next. Yup, he attended our intercessory group that very night and I got to share the dream with him. Spirit- normal! These occurrences will happen more frequently as you get closer to the Lord; it is not about you – it is about His kingdom – and Jesus is taking care of His people.

This scripture (Hab. 2:1-2) identifies four keys to hearing God's voice that Mark teaches:

1. I will stand my watch/post (wait in stillness, quiet your mind)
2. Keep watch to see (wait in a ready state of preparedness with confident expectation that you will hear the voice of the Lord)

3. Listen, and tune to flow (wait to hear what He will say to you, then listen for spontaneous thoughts)
4. Write it down (journaling is a journey)

We are all watchmen and the Lord has placed us in specific places in order to stand our guard because there is kingdom business to do! We are all watchmen and intercessors, every one of us, and we must prepare ourselves by quieting our minds (in stillness), then keep watch, listen, hear what the Lord has to say, and then write what you hear.

And now, perhaps the most frustrating part: **wait for *it***. It was many years before I could hear His voice again – and it took me an entire year (from 9/12/12 to 9/27/13) to hear in a spirit-normal manner. We have all been created by God the same way, with the ability to hear His voice which He desires more than anything, so there is no reason why God will not speak to you as He did to Mark or me. Our primary hindrance is the flesh; we must die to self because we cannot have it both ways. We must surrender our agendas, preconceived notions, and the fleshly cares of this world, which are (in part) based upon personal preferences, worldly ideas, and institutionalized religious doctrines. We need to silence all the thoughts waging battle in our mind, such as the lies of the enemy to deceive us with messages of doubt or fear by family members or friends who do not yet comprehend why we love Jesus so much.

If we want to hear God's voice, then we need to listen on His terms, not ours.

It is not your kingdom that God wants to talk to you about.

Waiting is literally… the art and science of getting perfectly quiet and remaining perfectly still.

It should seem clear to readers by now that the voice of God is not a sound that we can hear, nor is it a sound at all. The voice of God is a thought – it is a spontaneous thought that you did not manufacture, neither did it originate from anyone else. I will explain this in more detail later.

> "Teach me, Lord, to sort through the noises of this world to hear and discern Your powerful, wonderful, pure, precious voice." Priscilla Shirer

The noise pollution of this world is one of the weapons the enemy uses against us to distract us and disorient us – to prevent listeners from hearing God's truth and His message for us.

Now, I mentioned before that I struggle with "Restless Mind Syndrome." This is not an "official" medical term, as I have gone to many doctors and also searched the internet without success. I explained to them how my thoughts will not turn off or "be quiet" when I begin to pray or when I go to sleep at night, which resulted in insomnia for 15 years. When I pray in the Spirit, I want to hear God's voice, but the background chatter in my mind left me spiritually frustrated. Even if I was hearing His voice, I was never confident beyond the shadow of any doubt that it was God; it might be me or, worse, the enemy. So, I hope these tips may help.

Quiet Your Restless Mind[11]

Be Still

1. Be still. Be not preoccupied. Be not encumbered by the list of many things. Don't do, just be.
2. Let it all go. Nothing else really matters. Everything belongs to God anyway, so let it all go. To worry is to hold onto. It is not yours, so let it go. (Psalm 24)
3. The Lord is God. He's got it. It is all under His control. So let go of any fears or anxieties. You will not add one minute to your life by worrying (Matt. 6:25-34). In reality, the opposite is true – worry reduces your life expectancy.

---

[11] This message with 37 points was written in one sitting as I was listening in the flow of the Spirit's voice.

4. You cannot change anything except yourself. It is foolish to believe otherwise. Live your life according to the change within; then, perhaps, others will listen.
5. There is power, but the power is not of you. The power is being released in you by the Holy Spirit. Even your life-breath is a gift. Your heart beats 72-times minute without your permission, your purpose-driven will or self determination.
6. Your life is not your own. You were purchased for a price and it cost Jesus His life. He already saved you, so why are you so intent to re-save yourself with human effort; why do you strive? (Isa. 45:9) Be responsible, but live graciously (according to grace).
7. Nothing is so important that it cannot wait 30 minutes. It will still be there tomorrow. Life does not depend upon you; rather, you depend upon life. This world will go on without you as it has for 6,000 years. Wait 30 minutes – abide in the Life.
8. Do not worry. Worry is idolatry. Wonder instead. God is full of power and awe, so meditate on His awesome character – of wonder, beauty, and majesty.
9. If you still have random thoughts, then tell God, "thank you, thank you, thank you" over and over. Do it until you hear nothing, even if it takes 10 minutes or an hour. Gratitude is a spiritual discipline. Sometimes, an attitude of thanksgiving is all that it takes to open heaven's gate.
10. You are not alone. God is always with you. God is near. He may be silent, but He is always near to you.
11. Repent of any sin. Unconfessed sin stifles the flow of communion and hinders communication with God. Come to God with a clean (clear) heart.
12. Conversation is not prayer. Prayer is talking *to* God (one way); conversation involves listening *and* hearing (two way).

Be Quiet

13. Stop the noise. Turn off all sounds. They are distracting.

14. If necessary, turn on white noise to drown out all other sounds. Every sound stimulates a thought, which may trigger a reaction. Rob the ears of any noise; wear ear plugs.
15. If you can still sense things that distract you, such as light with your eyes closed, then wear a sleeping mask to block all light. Eliminate all distractions (or as many as possible). Stillness is what you seek.
16. Feel the stillness in your breath. It is quiet but it is still productive; it keeps you alive. Can you hear your breathing? If yes, then breathe slower and more gently until you hear nothing. Feel the air as it leaves your body when it does not make a sound. Stillness is now happening all around you. Stillness is more silent than quiet. Stillness is extra-quiet silence; stillness is the absence of all sound – and this is when I know that I am in God's presence.
17. Listen for the far away sound. It is like listening for the sound of a train whistle many miles away – or the chirp of a solitary cricket. It is like listening for the keys in the door. You will hear it because you expect to hear it. You know it can happen and you know that God is there, so believe that it will happen. Do not doubt. We were all created with the ability to hear God's voice. He created us – and we were created with this ability.

Be Yourself

18. Don't try to be someone you're not. Don't try to be what someone else told you to be. Be who you are. God created you unique. Even all your idiosyncrasies represent the specialness of who you are. Let you be you – and let them be them. God loves you just the way you are. You are intentional – just as God intended, so stop trying to be something that you are not. Just be you… and let God be God in you.
19. Relax. This is not a test. (Everybody passes)
20. Speak normal, listen normal, with quiet thoughts to the Lord. Be normal. Don't pretend to be pious. Just be yourself. God already knows everything about you. He

already knows your thoughts from far off. To pretend is to offend.
21. Get real. Half our struggle is trying to be what others want us to be. This is disingenuous to God. He knows when you are faking it.
22. Be honest with yourself. You may be able to fool or impress others, but no one can fool the inner man – or Him who created you as soul and spirit.
23. Don't rationalize or justify any sin. God knows your heart. He knows the motivation of your heart. He searches your heart. Nothing is hidden from Him. Just because He has not revealed your sin to anyone else or made you pay the penalty you deserve is not because He doesn't know – it is because God is merciful. Tell the truth.

Be Empty

24. Do you want to talk to God because you need something, or do you want to hear His voice? Do you love God or do you love His things? Tell Him. Surrender your prayer list; surrender your petitions. Would you want to have a relationship with someone who only befriended you because they wanted something from you?
25. Want nothing.
26. Desire only one thing – a deeper personal relationship with Jesus.
27. Call His name. He loves to hear His name as much as you do. It is like walking down a busy street to hear someone calling your name from behind. How precious is the sound of your name! You will stop, turn, listen and search for the origin of the sound until you find whoever is calling your name. The same thing happens with God. He loves to hear us when we call His name.
28. Listen for His reply.
29. Wave your hand high up when you see Him. This is how friends typically greet one another.
30. The busyness of the street is now an inaudible hush that is moving around you. It does not affect you – it is as if you do not exist as it moves around you. God is in this

moment. Nothing else matters. You are in His Presence. This is the most important moment of your life. God is here in the quiet and the stillness.

Hear Him!

31. Continue to be still – and wait for it.

Focus on the Moment

32. Distractions happen. Bathroom breaks happen. Phones may ring, so turn them to "silent." God is still going to be there when you get back. He never left; you did.
33. Wait for it.
34. Listen for a new thought. If you are not thinking it, then it comes from one of three sources: God, Satan, or other people. The longer you practice listening, the more able you are to hear His voice, discern His voice, and tune out the other voices. Yes, we can hear what other people are thinking – and sometimes they are in our head. They are not who you want to listen to at this time, so hang up. Perhaps they will leave a message or call back later ☺.
35. You are listening for new thoughts that you did not think or create. It may be God, so write it down. If you keep it in your head, the circus noise of daily cares will cause you to forget what you heard. We hear God with our mind. The mind can have thousands of thoughts an hour; you are listening to hear one. Wait for it.
36. You will hear many little thoughts from God. After a while, the sound becomes clearer. You are now able to discern God's voice.
37. Just wait until His voice pierces the silence. This is unmistakable. You will know that you know that you know. It is crystal clear, yet indescribable at the same time. Yup… you just heard His voice. You will never, ever, be able to unhear those words. They are etched in your soul; you will never forget those words. That is the power of hearing His voice; you can never unhear them. They will always remain with you. Even if you forget, the Holy Spirit who dwells in you will bring it to your remembrance, for His words are life-giving… and they are spirit and life.

Listening to hear God's voice is not a sprint – it is a marathon for disciples. We need to discipline our mental thoughts and heartfelt emotions every moment of every day to make them captive in obedience to Christ. I have often found that, while I am striving to hear His voice because I need an answer from Him, I discover two things: 1) He answers the questions I wasn't asking, and 2) He responds more to my yearning for Him than my desire to satisfy my personal answer-seeking agenda.

Listening is neither a shopping list of needs – nor an SOS. The Lord will talk to you about what He wants to talk to you about, but most of all, the Lord wants to have a relationship with you.

Jesus wants to have a relationship with you – and this is by way of a conversation. Jesus already knows what you need as well as the thoughts in your heart, so why try to impress upon Him your agenda. Jesus said, "Take My yoke upon you – and learn from Me" (Matt. 11:29). Listen to His words of life for you, set aside your distractions and press into a deeper relationship with Him.

> "Seek ye first the kingdom of God – and His righteousness [Jesus] – and all else will be taken care of" (Matt. 6:33)

If your mind continues to be overactive, and this happens to me quite often, I settle down into a quiet, comfortable spot and simply focus my thoughts upon Jesus; I think about and meditate upon Jesus, how wonderful He is and how much I love Him, and say thank you, thank you, thank you, over and over, sometimes for many minutes and even as long as an hour. Remember this: praise and thanksgiving opens the door of the divine.

If for any reason you still cannot hear after much meditation and prayerful waiting, then I suggest offering yourself as a living sacrifice upon the altar of His kingdom and ask the Lord to take all your cares for this life and to leave only those things that draw you closer to Him (Rom. 12:1, 2). If silence continues to happen, ask the Lord what, if anything, may be preventing you from hearing

His voice. Sometimes, the problem is us, and sometimes, we may be in testing.

One day, I was fully expecting to get a word from Him, but all I heard was silence. I stayed in quiet repose for three full hours without even as much as a flinch, but still... nothing. The next day, the Lord began talking again as He usually does, so I asked Him what the previous day was all about; why couldn't I hear His voice? He then told me – it was a test. He was testing my character and He wanted to see what my reaction was going to be; specifically, He wanted to see if I would bring a charge against Him after He indicated He was going to speak, but didn't. He wanted to see if I would raise my hand against Him in any manner. He wanted to teach me that, regardless of what happens, whether good or bad, whether in silence of in the multitude of divine thoughts, I am to reverence Him in all things. Wow!

> "LORD, what is man, that You take knowledge of him? Or the son of man, that You are mindful of him?" (Psa. 114:3) "That You should visit him every morning, and test him every moment?" (Job 7:18)

Sometimes life seems like nothing more than one continuous test to see if we are willing to listen for His voice and be guided by the Spirit. Oneness is what God desires more than anything – not sacrifices or obedience or any other programs, doctrines or ordinances. God desires intimacy where there is no separation between us and Him – in the love of God.

These steps may be used as guided meditation, but they are intended to become spiritual disciplines for living every day as unto the Lord. I am listening every moment of every day to hear His voice, as I walk and as I drive, and as often as possible without music or any other distractions, yet I always go back to one special chair to get still and hear God's voice. His presence is precious to me.

Truly, His Presence is heaven to me.

Listening is not something you do for God; it is the thing you do because this is who you are. You are in a relationship with who He is, not what you want. It is not something you *have* to do; it is something you *want* to do… and nothing can take the place of hearing His voice. Nothing!

One Final Step

After you have heard His voice, thank Him. Praise Him! Praise and thanksgiving will transition into worship and adoration – whereby "God is enthroned on the praises of His people." God is searching to and fro over all the earth for one thing: worshippers (John 4: 23, 24). God desires true worship, from a heart of joyful praise and thanksgiving. In this, the Lord is glorified.

Other Steps To Hearing

It is important to understand that some people will read this information but will still be unable to hear. That is ok, that is, if there is nothing hindering your ability to hear (such as unconfessed sin). Don't beat yourself up because sometimes listening takes a long time before hearing anything. It took me a year.

These steps, or any other steps, represent the hearing experience from one person's perspective. We are all different, so don't think you are doing something wrong if you haven't heard. Let me encourage you in this: I just found a journal entry I wrote on listening back in 1992 (22 years earlier). I was listening back then and heard His unmistakable voice, but life got busy, then complicated, then feverishly busy, and then…my journal to myself told me I had grown dull of hearing. I had been crying out to the Lord for guidance and direction even after hearing His voice for many years; I had been praying, "Here I am," and I had been crying out, "Turn Your ear to me" and then, one day, after I had been praying intently like this, I heard His voice again. Here is the closing paragraph of this 4-page journal from 22 years ago:

"When God has a plan for your life, sometimes you have to let go of your understanding. Proverbs 3:5,6 "Trust in the Lord with all your heart, and lean not on your own understanding." Sometimes I think it would have been easier for the Lord to have given us a "wake-up" button so He could get our attention. Don't let this little morsel pass you by. There isn't any problem on the Lord's end to hear us: the problem is on our end to hear Him. Keep busy, do lots of charitable work and volunteer on lots of committees, but sometimes He just wants to spend time talking with us instead of chasing us around between meetings. God is Lord of everything, including the Daytimer. Tomorrow may be the day you don't need to keep any of those appointments except the one He tried to tell you about for several months; "If you hear His voice, harden not your hearts."

I was humbled. I immediately went to my knees and asked for His forgiveness.

It is so easy to get off track. Just a slight deviation can put you miles off course within a short period of time. Stay focused on Jesus; keep your eyes on Him!

Ears For Ministry

You *can* hear the God's voice. It is very important to hear, especially if you are seeking truth about what you should do (as in a ministry call), so here are some other listening steps if you need more assistance:[12]

1. We must be ready to pray – always.
2. If it is very important, God may speak to us through other people, but *only* to confirm what He said to you. On important matters, we can expect – we must expect – God to talk to us personally.
3. Keep everything on the altar. If you get proud, God cannot use you.

---

[12] The source of these lecture notes was not documented, so I apologize in advance for using them without permission.

4. We can hear more clearly if we come to Him with a pure heart.
5. Do not tell people about your visions until you understand them.
6. Sometimes pipe dreams may become a reality (thoughts may come from out of the blue – but wait for confirmation)
7. The Lord gives chapter and verse from the Bible – God also speaks through His written word.
8. The Three Wise Men Principle (be wise, seek the Lord, adore Him – not the calling)
9. The Lord will lead us into victory, but success itself is the most dangerous obstacle to hearing His voice. Don't glory in success; focus on Jesus; delight yourself in the Lord.
10. Sometimes the Lord will lead us down a path that ends. Death to a vision is not the end of a promise spoken over you; this is a learning process to hear His voice – and to do what He says. We will be tested and we will face trials of many kinds, so remain faithful.
11. If you get lost, remember the axe-head principle: go back to the last place where you knew you heard from God (where you left the axe in the tree).
12. Consider the perspective principle: continue to check your life's ongoing confirmation against your original call – and look for road-signs.
13. Even if we fail, God does not take back His gifts or His calling. He waits patiently for us to come to our senses – and come back to Him with yielded hearts that are clean.
14. The second-best test is the guidance principle: does it bring us closer to God? Does it bring His people who are involved one step closer to freedom and maturity in the Lord?
15. The twin-natured principle: Love the Lord, love your neighbor; serve the Lord, serve your neighbor.
16. Does God get all the glory? This is the best-test to get on track and stay focused.

Guidance is, first of all, a relationship with the Guide. Some problems with Divine guidance:

1. We focus more on the work being done than on Jesus.
2. Sometimes the glory is so spectacular that the glory attaches itself to the work and not to the Lord. God never anoints ministries; He anoints people to do His will. He establishes everything for one purpose: to bring glory unto Himself!
3. If we make wrong choices, we can also end up robbing God, not only of His glory, but also of His rightful "first attention." (Don't be sidetracked by things of seemingly greater importance. Do what you know God wants you to do – and do it *first*!)
4. The enemy will often entice us with "many" good works to do in order to keep us from focusing on <u>one</u> "greater work" that Jesus predestined us to accomplish.

Be Ready to Listen

How do you know you have heard the truth? The word of God may come to you through the hearing of the ears or seeing with the eyes or as an understanding. We are all familiar with the scripture, "Faith comes by hearing, and hearing by the word of God" (Rom. 10:17), so, describe the word of God that came to you and how did you hear it? Was the word preached during a Sunday sermon or was it by reading the written Word of God? This is very important. There is a big difference between the <u>w</u>ord of God and "the <u>W</u>ord of God" (capital "W"). For most Bible-believing, born anew Christians, the image of our Bible pops into our mind when we read "the word." Certainly, we have all received truth through the Scriptures, but that does not mean we have heard "the word." This, therefore, is the big distinction between "sheep" who hear His voice and the "field" of your heart that hears but does not understand. Hearing is dependent upon understanding the message that you heard which comes from "the Word of God" Himself, Jesus Christ (Rev. 19:13).

The literal Greek for Romans 10:17 is: "Then – faith [is] from hearing, and the hearing through a *word* of/from Christ."

This *"word" rhema* – is a spoken word (utterance). Is Christ speaking to us – or – are we so wrapped up in the written word of God that we really do not need to – or want to – hear His voice? I am afraid the institutional church is repeating the sins of Israel; they have put the Word of God as like a law before men, whereby they must obey every jot and tittle of the Word, but meanwhile, they are missing the "Word of God" in the message. The institutional church seems to have created an idol of the written word that is preventing us from hearing the voice (word) of Christ; it must not become a substitute for hearing His voice. And what do we call anything that separates us from a personal relationship with God? Yes… it is called sin.

"My sheep hear My voice, and I know them, and they follow Me." Jesus desires to speak to each and every one of us on a personal level, to speak truth and life, but – do you have ears to hear?

The very Scriptures that were supposed to draw us closer to Christ may now be separating us from having a true, intimate, personal relationship with Christ. In this regard, fundamentalism is destroying the church of Jesus Christ by teaching the sheep to read with their eyes rather than hear with their spiritual ears. How can you have a relationship with any person if you do not communicate with them? Do idols or books talk to men? Do they listen (1 Kings 18:24-29)? Does your Bible listen to you? The Bible speaks to us in one way, but it does not engage in two-way communication… yet the Holy Spirit does! It is as if God is saying in this moment, "It has been a long time since you heard My Voice. Let's have a conversation… just you and Me."

Have we come again to become enslaved to the written word (law) which kills?

> "[God] who also made us sufficient as ministers of the new covenant, not of the letter but of the Spirit; for the letter kills, but the Spirit gives life" (2 Cor. 3:6).

> "This only I want to learn from you: did you receive the Spirit by the works of the law, or by the hearing of faith? Are you so foolish? Having begun in the Spirit, are you now being made perfect by the flesh?" (Gal. 3:2, 3) "But now after you have known God, or rather are known by God, how is it that you turn again to the weak and beggarly elements, to which you desire [new again] to be in bondage" (Gal. 4:9).

O foolish church, having begun in the Spirit – are we now attempting to fulfill our destiny in Christ by trusting in "the word of God" without needing to hear His voice? How can you have a personal relationship with a book? Indeed, yet that is what we do on Sundays. We proudly carry our leather-bound Swords with us into church and turn to chapter and verse as directed. Then we bow our heads, say Amen, and then go back to hearing our thoughts and promulgating our kingdom. We are ever listening (passively), but never hearing (attentively). Anathema!

Jesus is not looking for passive admirers – but devoted followers and disciples who listen!

> "You have neither heard His [the Father's] voice at any time, nor seen His form. [38] But you do not have His word abiding in you, because whom He sent, Him you do not believe. [39] You search the Scriptures, for *in them* you think you have eternal life" (John 5:37-39

One thing I ask: did you come to the knowledge of the truth (believe) by the Word or by the Spirit? Are you trying once again to accomplish in the flesh what began in the Spirit? Are we repeating the sins of our forefathers at the mountain who did not want to hear His voice? There are many teachers who claim the scriptures are the final authority of God's word and teach that God has ceased speaking and operating in spiritual gifts since the scriptures were codified. Huh? Since when has the Lord ever stopped speaking and bringing revelation to His people...

In Summary – my thoughts on hearing God's voice:

- Be attentive – always listen continuously
- Come into His presence – with an open mind and a clear heart
- Walk in faith – being thoroughly persuaded and convinced
- Hear – listen to hear the *rhema* (utterance) voice of the Lord
- Obey – listen intelligently
- Hear and understand – *akouo* perceive His voice with the *noeo* mind and hide His words in your heart
- Hear and obey – *shema*
- Come, let us reason together – talk with the Lord on His terms; have times of conversation
- Know and understand – a complete understanding that results in an *oida* personal relationship
- Call upon the name of the Lord – proclaim "our God reigns"

To Listen Anew

Jesus told us, "Unless one is born anew, he cannot perceive the kingdom of God" (John 3:3). And so, the message of "being born again" is quite pervasive within the Christian tradition; however, Jesus is teaching us much truth within these few verses of scripture.

Jesus is teaching us deep truth and we need to listen attentively to hear what He is saying; Jesus is teaching us, by telling us – to understand. The word translated "see" is '*oida*' (1492) and means, "to know completely and absolutely, to see, *to perceive – and understand.*" This is one of sixteen words that are translated 'understand' in the scriptures – and it carries with it the strongest meaning of all. This is not simply '*ginosko*' knowing that comes by way of experience or observation; '*oida*' implies knowing in the fullest sense with a thorough completeness of understanding in a personal, relational, experiential manner – to comprehend.

Literally, "unless one is born anew from above, he cannot comprehend the kingdom of God." We cannot see or understand the kingdom of God unless we have been born anew by the Spirit.

It stands to reason, then, that unless someone is born anew, they cannot understand the kingdom – or hear the Lord's voice. This, my friends, is Faith 101 and our point of origin in the kingdom for those who are saved.

Jesus wants us to fully understand and comprehend the kingdom of God, but this is *only* possible as a born anew person according to the Spirit. Nicodemus did not grasp this concept, somehow thinking he needed to be *'deuteros'* – born a second time. However, Jesus tells us, "We must be born of water and the Spirit" (v.5) whereby the Spirit must give birth to us, but is this literal or figurative language? I can assure you, that in one of the most important messages by Jesus Himself – He is being quite literal, and He is leaving no room for equivocation or misunderstanding!

We must be born of the Spirit! This act alone enables us to experience the kingdom of heaven, and therefore, there are no other means available for such a salvation. The Spirit is Life!

Pay close attention! We cannot believe in the born anew spirit-life until we have come to terms with the water-life. *We cannot live two lives within the same body*; either we will love the one or hate the other. We cannot serve the Lord single-heartedly if we are living *double-minded* (*dipsuchos* – literally, two-souled); nor can we serve the Lord in spirit and in truth if we have not allowed our mind to be sanctified by the Spirit of truth. The water-life must die before the Spirit-life can live; we must become dead in the water, if you will (a type of baptism) in order to live according to the Spirit-directed life. There is only one way to live the Spirit-directed life, and this requires us to die to self, to place ourselves on the altar as a living sacrifice (Rom. 12), to abandon the kingdom of our self-directed water-life, to render ourselves dead to the cares of this world, and then let the Spirit birth us into the kingdom. Then, and only then, are we raised (resurrected) to newness of life according to the Spirit of life in Christ Jesus. The water-man must yield to the spirit-man. The old man must be put to death, *by us*, so that the new man can be raised to newness of life, by the Spirit. This is how we are birthed anew by the Spirit. One water birth, one life and one death; then one new birth, a new spirit, one Spirit, one way and one truth, in oneness through newness, with life anew – with Jesus only, in oneness with the Father!

And Jesus anticipated the very next thought by Nicodemus, as well as you and me, when He says, "Do not marvel (be amazed) that I said to you, "You must be born anew (*anothen*, from above; v.7)." Jesus has just spoken the same truth twice and the very next thing He says comes like a deep crescendo of truth that reverberates understanding in which most readers of gospel truth somehow miss.

> "The wind blows where it wishes, and you hear the sound of it, but cannot *tell* (*oida – understand*) where it comes from and where it goes. So is everyone who is born of the Spirit" (v.8)

Literally, "The wind blows… and you hear it… but you cannot understand where the Spirit comes from or what He does or where He goes" unless you are birthed anew by the Spirit of God!!! *If you read only one truth within all the messages that I write, read this passage with the desire to **completely and thoroughly comprehend this truth**, as it pertains to hearing God's voice or seeing spiritual truth: **you must be born anew by the Spirit of God to understand how the kingdom of God operates**!*

Jesus is telling Nicodemus (and also you and me) that we can experientially hear the sound of it (the flow of the Spirit) and see how it moves physical things like tree leaves (and hearts), but we may not '*akouo*' be able to hear with understanding; otherwise, we should "see" '*oida*' where this sound is coming from and we could "tell" '*oida*' know and completely understand Who is speaking to us. Hearing the Lord's utterance is not a sound that is heard any more than it is something that can be seen or felt, but rather… it is a Divine Thought!

And the response by Nicodemus is very similar to millions of believers who have been taught the truth of Jesus from an institutional religious perspective: "How can these things be?" (v.9)

The principle point of hearing is to understand. Period!

Jesus came to teach us one thing: to understand – the kingdom of God is within you! Understand!!! "The kingdom of heaven is at hand." Again and again, Jesus taught us the divine relationship comes by hearing with understanding and seeing with perceiving, which cannot happen apart from the birthing anew by the Spirit.

"The kingdom of God is within you" (Luke 17:21).

The first birthing of water is our baptism into this world, but the birthing of the Spirit is our baptism into the heavenly kingdom of God – and this is done through a gateway as well, through a Door called Jesus Christ (John 10:7-9). The new birth of the Spirit offers people a second life to live; this is not a second chance to live again in the manner of the old self with better upgrades, but to be born anew, from above, and to live eternally as we were intended to live, as spiritual beings clothed in human flesh upon the earth, whereby we are given a new heart and a new spirit in order to live life on the earth in the manner in which God originally planned: according to the Spirit (Ezek. 36:27, 27). The new spirit within us – is being guided and directed by the Holy Spirit who comes along side us to teach us ways everlasting – every step of the way! Our thoughts are temporal, but the Lord's thoughts and utterances are eternal!

This is eternal life! Any other '*heteros*' gospel is not the gospel of grace and truth!

If this comes to you as a new teaching about the reason why Jesus came to earth, then let me remind you that Jesus said, "I am the

Way, the Truth and the Life. No one comes to the Father…….. but by way of Me." Jesus wants us to understand the totality of who He is and to understand Him, as the One who '*oida*' completely comprehends – whereby Jesus brings understanding to us. This is the nature of the divine relationship that the Father desires for everyine: to *oida* hear and *oida* see and *oida* comprehend His thoughts and ways, just as Jesus lived in *oida* oneness with the Father.

Jesus did not tell us to pray the sinner's prayer or to believe and be baptized, not that any of these are wrong as elemental teachings about salvation, but Jesus simply said… "you MUST be born anew" by the Spirit. Period! The implication here is dynamic and magnificent, so as to convert us from what we were – to become changed into what we were meant to be – from that which is flesh-constrained into that which is spirit-ordained. We must be birthed anew by the Spirit if we want to experience the kingdom of heaven. This is a spiritual paradigm change whereby we are converted from the focus on self and any other kingdom according to the flesh – to focus upon Jesus and His kingdom according to the Spirit dwelling within us (John 14:17; Rom. 8:11).

Hey, but doesn't this conflict with the teaching by Jesus when he was asked, "What must I do to be saved?" (Luke 10:25). No, not at all. In three separate accounts by three gospel writers, all writing from three different perspectives, the truth is given very clearly: "**_Hear, O Israel_**… love the Lord with all your heart, soul, mind and strength, and the second is like it… love your neighbor as yourself" (Matt. 22:39; Mark 12:29; Luke 10:27; Deut. 6:5; Lev. 19:18; also known as the royal law, the law of love – James 2:8).

Foremost, in priority firsts is this: **_Hear_**! We cannot go any further unless we can hear.

Now then, let's pay very careful attention to one of four words; the word for mind is '*dianoia*' and means, "to thoroughly think through, to know, deep meditative thoughts resulting in completeness of understanding."[13] If '*oida*' is having the complete understanding as coming from an intimate personal experience, then '*dianoia*' is the understanding that comes thoroughly complete – in unity and oneness of heart and mind (as elements of the soul) as a working of grace by the Spirit within a person's spirit (your inner spirit-man where the kingdom of God resides, by grace through faith).

The Holy Spirit has been upon the earth the entire time, hovering, and it is the Spirit who guides us into the knowledge of the truth (John 16:13). The Spirit is life and the Spirit is truth. The Spirit shows us the way because He is the Doorkeeper for the Door (John 10:3), and once we have entered into the divine relationship with Jesus, the Holy Spirit transforms us, over and over, and renews our minds, over and over, until we attain the full measure of Christ within us (maturity) and we bear fruit consistent with the message abiding within us. This is the result of the birthing of the Spirit, whereby we can tell, by examining our fruit, if we belong to Jesus or not, and whereby we may '*oida*' see the kingdom of God with the eyes of our understanding (Eph. 3:17), and whereby, from conception to maturity, the Holy Spirit becomes our seal of authenticity (of Christ's ownership) on the day of salvation.

If this is true, then why did Jesus tell us He had to go away so that He could send the Holy Spirit? So glad you asked. The Spirit was never sent away; the Spirit has always been beside us every moment of every day, but a new dimension of the Spirit was sent into the church age to impart spiritual gifts and release divine power for one reason: for the building of faithful hearers and followers into "a" church as the bride of Christ.

There are no conflicts or contradictions in the messages intended for attaining salvation… only different perspectives – and all are equally applicable. At the risk of total redundancy – the Spirit, the Spirit, the Spirit!!! If you want to understand, then be born anew as a working of the Spirit! If you still have questions concerning salvation, then ask Him yourself.

---

[13] Strong's Concordance.

If you have truly been born of the Spirit, then do what the Spirit says – and live life as a spiritual being – and allow the Spirit who birthed you to conform you into the likeness (exact impress) of Jesus by understanding His message – and then do what He tells you. Anything less is just spiritual gamesmanship – lacking the substance of *oida* faith, *oida* obedience and *oida* understanding that results in eternal life in the kingdom of God.

Not long ago, I heard a sermon about a rope on a mountain from two perspectives: rock climbing versus rappelling. For the rock climber, the rope is there – just in case; for rappelling, it is all about the rope. The climber sees the rope as an "I got this" safety measure, while the other fully understands this endeavor is impossible without the rope. If the Holy Spirit is the rope, who was sent as the Paraclete to come alongside us and guide us at all times, then how do you see Him… as one who assists your program to ascend – or as one who becomes your source for survival?

If I could give the Bible a subtitle, it would be: The Sojourners Manual for Understanding. It seems, upon much reflection and meditation – that "understanding" is one of the seven golden threads contained within this book of love between our heavenly Father and His children. God wants us to know His thoughts and know His ways – *God wants us to understand.*

And Jesus came to teach us the truth, and to show the way of understanding – as The Way.

We cannot hear God's voice – nor can we see the kingdom – without the Spirit. If you want to hear God's voice in a relational manner, then you must be born anew by the Spirit. Apart from the Spirit, we can do nothing – and know even less (1 Cor. 2:6; 8:2). There is NO other way!

Ginosko and *Oida*

Let us examine the relationship between *ginosko* knowing and *oida* understanding that was initially presented in Regenesis, Chapter 7, p. 244-246.

How are we ever going to understand who God is if we don't know the scriptures or if we selectively choose which scriptures are valid? And worse even, to know them without instrumental help, empowering or enlightenment from the Holy Spirit? What good is knowledge apart from the Holy Spirit who is truth (1 John 5:6)? Jesus struggled to convey this very issue regarding Jewish leaders who claimed to know the truth, but did not know God.

> "Yet you have not known Him (*ginosko*), but I know Him (*oida*). And if I say, 'I do not know (*oida*) Him,' I shall be a liar like you; but I do know Him (*oida*) and keep His word" (John 8:55).

Jesus is telling us that He knows *and* understands (*oida*) the Father perfectly, completely, even intimately, but these Jewish leaders only know of God (*ginosko*) as a mental construct, from a perspective not based upon personal experience resulting in a personal relationship. Jesus fully perceives and comprehends the Father; in contrast, the leaders only know Him anecdotally. Jesus was not just teaching them thoughts, words and concepts about the Father, He was revealing the Father to them hoping they would understand, comprehend – and perceive.

> "Then they said to Him, "Where is Your Father?" Jesus answered, "You know (*oida*) neither Me nor My Father. If you had known (*oida*) Me, you would have known (*oida*) My Father also" (John 8:19).

> "Jesus answered and said to him, "What I am doing you do not understand (*oida*) now, but you will know (*ginosko*) after this" (John 13:7).

> "If you had known (*ginosko*) Me, you would have
> known (*oida*) My Father also; and from now on you
> know (*ginosko*) Him and have seen (3708 beheld)
> Him." (John 14:7)

> "the Spirit of truth, whom the world cannot receive,
> because it neither sees Him nor knows (*ginosko*)
> Him; but you (*disciples*) know (*oida*) Him, for He
> dwells with you and will be in you" (John 14:17;
> *italics* by author).

There is a tremendous difference between knowing, understanding and comprehending. To know is superficial and primarily fact-based information, knowledge in the abstract. To understand is based upon first-hand observation, experience and application. Comprehension is based upon perception involving reflective and meditative thoughts of a deep, personal nature that are rooted in an intimate, experiential relationship. Do you "*ginoska*" God or do you "*oida*" Him? The Father wants you to "*oida*" Him! We need to move past the essence of knowing into the substance of experiential comprehension. We must perceive God with an understanding mind (*nous*) on a personal level! For this to occur, we need the Holy Spirit of God.

> "None of them shall teach his neighbor, and none
> his brother, saying, 'Know the LORD (*ginosko*),' for
> all shall know (*oida*) Me, from the least of them to
> the greatest of them" (Heb. 8:11; Jer. 31:34).

This is what the Lord desires: for all of us to experience the Lord of glory in a personal, experiential manner resulting in a personal *oida* relationship being thoroughly persuaded and confident through faith that leads to deep, relational understanding – into perceiving God for who He is.

> "For what man knows (*oida*) the things of a man
> except the spirit of the man which is in him? Even
> so no one knows (*ginosko*) the things of God except

the Spirit of God. [12] Now we have received, not the spirit of the world, but the Spirit who is from God, that we might know (*oida*) the things that have been freely given to us by God" (1 Cor. 2:11, 12).

Hear The Voice!

God wants us to hear His voice, the *rhema* (utterance) word of truth (from Him) so that we can understand the kingdom more and more. We are a kingdom of priests and prophets who have been activated for duty, as a people who hear His voice, who prophetically walk in faith and listen intelligently (obey). It is not enough to know the Lord (*ginosko*) or to know His word; the Lord Jesus is calling out to all the earth to gather together a people who will hear His voice – ***and understand the message*** – and follow Him. Jesus is seeking worshippers who want to worship Him (as a form of imitation) and live according to His ways, not as in the days of the rebellion (in the wilderness), nor as in the days of this current rebellion who teach all men to obey *written* words rather than experience *rhema* truth. Why do we fear the Holy Spirit? It is the Spirit that guides us and speaks truth to us so that we may hear His voice – and follow Jesus.

True disciples hear and follow – and these ones are called to proclaim "our God reigns." We are the people of His pasture – "My sheep hear My voice," and He has arranged us by the hearing of His voice. The Lord is arranging all things – because all things are His. The Lord will do what He wants with His things and He arranges them according to His purpose and plan. Our priestly duty is to hear His voice, understand what He says, and live as prophetic people who do not live unto themselves, but rather, as unto the Lord. We are being arranged. He is preparing His lampstands. The Lord is moving heaven and earth in preparation for the regeneration of all things. All things are being arranged – and then they will be shaken.

Do you know who you are and what your purpose in life is? Truly, we are here for the Lord's good pleasure and to declare His kingdom with Christ as King. We who hear His voice are being arranged and moved into position, to times and places that were appointed from the beginning. It is not about us – it is all about Jesus – and God gets the glory! Now is the time to hear His voice and prepare our hearts to understand what the Lord is speaking to us at this time. We have not been wandering around without a clue; we are sojourners who should be listening to hear His voice so as to fill the earth with the sound of His name and to proclaim His mighty works – past, present and future. A shout will go out across the land – and worldly kingdoms will crumble – and only the glory of the Lord will remain!

"Then men began to call on the name of the Lord" (Gen. 4:26) and men are still calling on the Lord today. We are here to proclaim! The verb "call" is '*qara*' (7121) meaning "to call out to, make proclamation, pronounce." We often interpret this word to be a calling out to God in a good manner, the inherent meaning "through the idea of accosting a person" is derived from the root word '*qara*' (7122) meaning, "to encounter, whether accidentally or *in a hostile manner*."[14]

We are calling on the Lord, whether accidentally or loudly or boldly, for Him to come alongside us and be with us as we sojourn through this planet. We are asking for His help to lead us and guide us through many of life's pitfalls and problems, and to rescue us when we succumb to fear or doubt or sin, yet there also remains an element of "the chance encounter" when we call on the Lord, that He may '*qirah and paga*' (7125, 6293) meet us where we are at – and respond to us (hear our call). Do we call on the Lord and expect to encounter Him in the midst of life, or do our prayers sound more like a "Hail Mary" pass into the end-zone? Have we become so detached from the Lord that we don't expect to encounter Him when we call out to Him?

The calling on "the name of the Lord" at this point (Gen. 4:26) is significant on several levels; it is first mentioned immediately after the birth of Enosh to Seth:

---

[14] Cross referencing terms and definitions from Strong's and Vines.

1. The lineage of man upon the earth is now firmly established with a grandson of Adam and Eve, despite our enemy's best efforts to thwart the invasion of man upon the earth through the death of Abel by Cain
2. Man will continue to inhabit the earth and fulfill the first commandment: have dominion
3. The name Enosh (583 from 582) means: man, a mortal, as a weak and dependent creature, which suggests the frailty, vulnerability and finitude of man – in contrast to "the Lord" (see Job 4:17; Psa. 103:14, 15)[15] and it is from this lineage that all men were born in weakness to be dependent upon the Spirit of God for all physical and spiritual assistance
4. The name of the Lord "*YHWH*" is mentioned again, as One who is known by Adam, as the same One that is Lord God who created the host of heaven and of earth (Gen. 2:1) and breathed into Adam the breath of life whereby he became a living soul (v.2:7).

When we forget to call upon the Lord, then we forget who He is and then we forget who we are – and then forget what we are supposed to do, and then we try to do it in our own human effort and will. We were never intended to live in this manner; we were created in weakness for a reason, as dependent creatures, to be utterly dependent upon the Lord as our strong help and Deliverer. The Lord wants us to partner *with* Him, as a working of His will, to co-deliver the earth from the bondage of Satan. So consider this: the first family knew how important it is to call upon the Lord… but do we? Is the Lord Jesus our first call before we even get into trouble, or is He a "last resort" when all our human efforts fail?

Adam knew His name, but God's chosen people would soon forget (fail to remember Him and fail to acknowledge Him), which we see when Moses asks the Lord for His name. It seems the Lord always wanted to reveal the fullness of His name and His nature *and* His will to man, so He gave us His official name "YHWH," but when we walk in doubt, soon followed by disobedience, fear

---

[15] Strong's

and unbelief, then the way and manner in which we live affects our understanding of "Who" the Lord God is. When we ask in ignorance "Who" the Lord is, then we might expect to get the same answer as Moses did: "I Am Who I Am" (Ex. 3:14). This is not a special name given specifically to Moses for the Exodus; this is His covenantal name for a wayward people He wants to have a personal relationship with (within the fullest expression of the divine relationship that abides in His presence which comes by way of hearing His voice). The Lord wants us to hear His *rhema* voice and to abide in His presence – daily!

Three things we must always remember about the Lord who loves us:

1. He is a living God who reveals Himself (as the God who exists)
2. He speaks to men to reveal His plans (as the God who effects His will)
3. He gives of Himself (Father, Son and Spirit) so that we may accomplish our mission (to know and understand Him within a personal relationship that is born of love, trust, faith and obedience)

When we call out to God in a friendship manner to come alongside us, then who might we also encounter in a hostile manner along this path of life? Yes, the deceiver himself, Satan, who is trying to separate us from the love of God! This is the same person who is bringing a charge against God's elect and condemns us (Rom. 8:33-35). We were sent to come against the kingdom of darkness with the light of God's truth in us and the Holy Spirit alongside us – and also by the word of our testimony concerning the testimony of Jesus flowing through us. When we go out and proclaim the name of the Lord, I can assure you this: we will "chance encounter" Satan in the midst of trials, temptation and tribulation, and we must accost Him with the word of our testimony and the name of Jesus, whereby we will also have a "chance encounter" with the Lord and remain in His presence. We were never meant to make it out of here alive, or unscathed by the ravages of sin; we were intended to be enjoined to the Spirit so as to walk in partnership with God to accomplish all that He planned according to His divine will.

> "And they shall call His name Emmanuel, which is translated, God *with* us" (Matt. 1:23).

The word "with" is '*meta*' (3326) meaning – "joined with, accompaniment amid" this sojourned life. From Enosh to Jesus to the Holy Spirit's presence today, we see God joined with us and *alongside us* every step of the way. He knows that we are dust and He knows fully the predicament we are in before we even call upon His name – because He is *right there beside us* and dwelling within us every step of the way. Saints, we can take great solace in the '*paraklesis*' (3874) presence of God who tells us, "I will never leave you or forsake you" (Heb. 13:5).

The application of "to call upon" can be interpreted two ways; one for good and the other bad. When the Lord put a pillar of cloud between the Egyptians and the Israelites at the Sea of Reeds, both peoples 'encountered' the Lord; it caused illuminating light for the children of God, but this same cloud caused darkness upon the Egyptians. The more I come to know the Lord and the understanding of His thoughts and ways, this I have learned: the Lord can create something with dual purpose according to His will. To one person, it becomes a blessing, but for the other person, it becomes a curse. Type, antitype; agonist, antagonist; *dote* (give), antidote.

There are not two ends of the spectrum; there is one Spectrum, one truth and only one kingdom, but there may be multiple perspectives – it all depends upon which camp you are in: light or darkness. Your perspective affects the outcome of your life; for example, boiling water can soften potatoes or harden eggs… so it seems our outcome has more to do with what we are made of… than our circumstances.

And darkness hates light!

The events that caused Joseph to be sold into slavery by his brothers also had two perspectives, for Joseph said, "You meant it for evil, but God meant it for good." We must position ourselves to see earthly happenings from God's perspective. For this reason, I do not seek signs but rather the understanding that comes from knowing His way in a particular matter – and this wisdom comes from hearing His voice tell me His words of truth. I want to know truth from His perspective; and once I hear His truth on the matter – then I can proclaim His goodness!

When we call upon the name of the Lord, we are accomplishing two objectives: to come against the enemy – and also make bold proclamations: "OUR GOD REIGNS!" We were sent to have dominion over *all* the earth. We were not sent here to become captives of sin according to the kingdom of darkness or any other kingdom, including our own, or to hide in a foxhole. We were determined to be sent, from the beginning, but then 'the Garden incident' happened and we became bound in bondage, as captives of our rationalized, selfish way – and we ourselves needed to be delivered. We were sent to redeem the earth from darkness and deliver it to Lord Almighty – and this is still the plan, but we lost our way.

For too long we have called on the name of the Lord simply for divine assistance, but now a time is coming when we will call out His name and proclaim with a mighty shout, "OUR GOD REIGNS!" For His kingdom and His good pleasure, we will make bold proclamations for the tearing down of strongholds, for breakthrough, for deliverance of captives and for the healing of the nations. We are bringing light to the darkness and we will encounter this enemy; we will come "in the Spirit of our God" and come against this thief with truth. We are to gather together as many souls as will listen, to gather them together with His love so that He may wrap them in His grace – to advance His kingdom! We need to declare, testify, proclaim, witness and shout truth from the rooftops – and serve Him with one accord.

> "For then I will restore to the peoples a pure language, that they all may call on the name of the LORD, to serve Him with one accord" (Zeph. 3:9).

> "And it shall come to pass that whoever calls on the name of the LORD shall be saved. For in Mount Zion and in Jerusalem there shall be deliverance, as the LORD has said, among the remnant whom the LORD calls" (Joel 2:32).

Sifting, separating, dividing – and arranging. The Lord is doing it – and it is marvelous to comprehend. If you cannot hear His voice, then who do you think you are… just a human being? You are not *just* a human being, so stop using that excuse. You are a spiritual being that is having a human experience that was born with the ability to hear God's voice… but you stopped listening. Consider this: we will all be held accountable one way or the other, because the word has gone out and we are all without excuse, so why would we want to continue to test the Lord? Either way, it doesn't end well for those who refuse to listen.

Consider this: angels are messengers, from the Greek '*angelos*' meaning, "sent to deliver a message." Angels are spiritual beings from heaven who are sent to deliver messages to the sons of men in order to do the will of God. Likewise, the sons of men are spiritual beings who also were sent to earth to call on His name, proclaim messages and share the good news with other men, and though, being a little lower than angels, yet we have been crowned with glory and honor to become a likeness of Christ. The host of heaven and the host of earth are messengers for the Lord of Hosts – and the Lord of Hosts created us to be His messengers.

In order for us to be messengers of good news, we must be able to hear the voice of God for ourselves, understand what He is saying, and communicate with Him regarding His will that He wants to accomplish through us. The Lord is our Focus! Consider what the angel of the Lord said to John:

> "And I fell at his feet to worship him. But he said to me, "See that you do not do that! I am your fellow servant, *and of your brethren* who have the testimony of Jesus. Worship God! For the testimony of Jesus is the spirit of prophecy." (Rev. 19:10).

Angels are fellow servants *and our brethren* who also have the testimony of Jesus. Angels testify according to what they have been told, but we can also testify concerning what we have experienced.

The Conversation

Has anyone ever come up to you with the phrase, "have you got a minute?" Or perhaps, "can I have a word with you?" These are colloquialisms to mean: let's talk. This person wants to have a conversation with you. In much the same way, Jesus also wants to have a word with you. He is Lord of heaven and earth – and you – and He wants to tell us what He wants us to do, but do we have ears to hear? This is why we need to listen for His voice – and hear Him.

Many of us can quote Romans 10:17 and nearly all of us know it by heart. "So then, faith comes by hearing and hearing by the word of God." However, there is a difference in the literal Greek, which says,

> "Then – faith [is] from hearing, and the hearing through a word of Christ."

Most of us have been taught the translated meaning "by the word of God" refers to the scriptures, but this is wrong on two counts: 1) the 'word' here is *rhema*, an utterance, a spoken word, not the written word, and 2) these are the spoken word<u>s</u> (plural) of Christ. Jesus wants to have words with you! Jesus wants to communicate *rhema* words of truth *with* you.

There is also a subtle difference between "faith comes by hearing" and "faith is from hearing." Most preachers have taught us faith comes by hearing the gospel preached to us – and this is what the scriptures seem to teach us (v.10:14). Or do they? Are the scriptures teaching us to send preachers to preach the gospel or are they telling us to teach others to have a conversation with Christ? I believe these words indicate that we are to have a conversation with Christ. If faith comes by hearing, then faith is the primary article that originates from the teaching of men, but if faith *is* from hearing, then hearing is the primary article that originates from Christ to produce faith.

Hearing is the primary article – and hearing from Christ is the imperative.

His word has already gone out to all the world (Psa. 19:4; Rom. 10:18), so man's preaching is "already" secondary to the Spirit's Voice of Truth (the inner Witness) that has already spoken words of life and truth to every person on earth. And thus, the preacher and the church cannot be blamed if someone refuses to hear the message from the Spirit to repent – and believe.

Faith does not produce hearing, but rather, hearing His voice produces faith with obedience!

Faith is from hearing the voice of the Lord – period. "Who then, having heard, rebelled?" (Heb. 3:16). Faith is not the object; hearing the voice of Christ is! And this leads us into a divine relationship that results in divine service according to faith – by God's grace.

Faith becomes real to us once we have heard God's voice.

Our testimony is not based upon what we know – but – what we have experienced, seen and heard. Once you have heard His voice, I can assure you, you will never be able to unhear it. It is as if our soul latches onto it and treasures it more than anything else.

"Faith is the assurance... and the certainty" and "faith is from hearing" (Heb. 11:1; Rom. 10:17). Having been thoroughly persuaded and convinced, faith is the result of hearing the truth from the Voice of Truth (Jesus) through the Spirit of truth. We need to listen and hear His voice – if we are ever going to walk in truth according to the Spirit.

Some translations correctly locate the word "through" between 'hearing' and 'a word.' Thus, "Faith comes by hearing and hearing through a word of Christ" clearly puts the emphasis on "hearing" that comes "through a *rhema* word" from Christ. One translation erringly puts it like this: "Consequently, faith comes from hearing the message, and the message is heard through the word about Christ" (NIV – the Nearly Inspired Translation). Jesus does not want us to hear a message "about" Him; rather, He wants us to hear His voice and "have words with us." Hearing His voice is not extemporaneous, as if hearing a casual word or teaching about Christ makes you a believer. You cannot have a personal relationship with a message about Christ or a book about Christ; you must dine and recline with Christ Himself. Hearing a *rhema* utterance from Christ is a daily discipline for disciples to produce understanding.

The spirit of religion has inculcated us to only accept the written word of God as infallible (since sinful man is fallible). This spirit has also changed the definition of *'logos'* to be "the written word," thus minimizing "hearing" in order to elevate reading written words of scripture to near-worship status, and errantly claiming God only speaks to us through His written word with divine assistance from the Holy Spirit. The Bible now, in this regard, is like the golden calf; it is something that does not talk, we can control it, obedience by knowing is optional, and hearing the utterance of the Lord is, well, a relegated responsibility that is given to a duly appointed leader by a select group of people often resembling a minority mob.

From this point forward, we must not think simplistically about *logos* as the written word. It implies so much more (which we will discuss in depth a little later), but before we go any further, let us try to understand the meaning of logos as "the many ways God chooses to express Himself," not just as words written or spoken, but as expressions revealed to us as thoughts and utterances. And the fullest expression of God was revealed to us as *Logos*, Jesus Christ Himself (John 1:1).

The original manuscript is, indeed, infallible; however, there are no original manuscripts and, thus, there are numerous copies with manuscript additions and omissions, as well as translation errors. The apostle Paul is prone to using rhetorical questions to illuminate truth to us, but we often miss these unless we read the notes within the study Bible margin. There are words and colloquialisms used "back in the day" that we have to translate into modern meaning, and then there are modern terms and words which do not appear in the scriptures, like: Genesis, Bible study, personal, relationship, rapture, intimacy, reality, human, manage, Sunday school, control…" so, here are some words and terms that do occur:

"Conversation" is a word that only occurs twice in the NKJV and just twenty times in the KJV. This word seems to have changed meaning since first used – with implied behavior as well as the exchange of words. "And He said to them, "What kind of *conversation* (*logos*) is this that you have with one another as you walk and are [standing there] sad?" (Luke 24:17; [words added from the Greek]). The KJV translates it as "manner of communications." This is *logos* (3056) "a word, that which is spoken."[16] These disciples are on the road to Emmaus and are speaking to one another, using *logos* words with implied behavior, yet Jesus wants to have a conversation with them using *rhema* (utterance) words that leads to revelation and understanding – and that is exactly what happened moments later when He "opened their mind to understand" the Scriptures. The "ears of their mind" were opened, thus allowing the burning of revelation truth to become manifest in their hearts. Now, they "are" hearing. They heard the Voice of truth – then they perceived the truth in their heart.

---

[16] Vines Expository, communicate, #2, logos.

Let us contrast this same word in the Old Testament: "Then all the princes came to Jeremiah and asked him. And he told them according to all these words that the king had commanded. So, they stopped speaking with him, for the *conversation* had not been heard" (Jer. 38:27). Jeremiah spoke, the people stopped listening, and thus... the conversation was over – "for the matter was not *perceived*" (the word perceived is *"shama"* (8085) to listen intelligently). Can you picture the implied behavior? Arms folded across their chest, picking up something to read or looking elsewhere to distract them, eyes darting around the room; their behavior mimicking their conversation.

When we are listening, the Lord can tell by our implied behavior if we are listening passively or we desire to hear operationally, instructively, and attentively in order to gain understanding and perceive the thoughts and ways of the Lord.

Words of a Similar Meaning

There are a variety of words that we can use to capture the essence of communication, like conversation, dialogue, talking, speaking, oration, hearing, understanding, discourse.

The Greek word '*anastrophe*' (391) often translated as conversation, means: "behavior, conversation, life; to turn back, return (to the way you were); to move about in a place, **to sojourn and to conduct oneself, indicating one's manner of life and character to which you were called.**"[17]

This word embodies the essence of who we are as sojourners on earth. It is the evidence of living according to a belief that also exhibits our behavior and mannerisms; it is the outward expression of an inward reality manifested by our thoughts, words and implied behavior (doings) based upon your understanding of who you are according to who you were originally (being). You are a spiritual

---

[17] Vine's Expository, Behave, A.1, anastrepho (390). Also see Abide, Conversation, Life.

being having a human experience – and your life will either manifest the paradigm of faith or worldly submission according to your perspective of "who" you think you are. You can profess to know the truth so as to deceive yourself, but if you truly possess faith, then your life will reflect the truth of the scriptures – and your implied behavior will manifest the character of Christ Jesus. Thus, there are three kinds of believers: believers, non-believers and make-believers. Does your life resemble the character of Christ? If not, then perhaps it is time for conversion – and Divine communication.

By our mouth we will communicate the truth of who we are – from the inside out. Through our belief system, we will conduct ourselves – and our actions and behaviors will manifest our inward reality. This is the message Paul gave to Timothy (1 Tim. 3:15) and this is the message given to the local church (Eph. 2:3; 2 Cor. 1:12). This is the manner of life in which you live according to what you believe (Gal 1:13; Eph. 4:22; 1 Tim. 4:12; Heb. 13:7; James 3:13; 1 Pet. 1:15, 18; 2:12; 3:1, 2, 6; 2 Pet. 2:7; 3:11). [18]

Words are very powerful; they have inherent meaning when arranged in certain ways. When words are arranged, they convey a message, but sometimes the message is lost between the words. Which Bible translation is most accurate? Well, now we are getting off point.

The focus here is not the written word but the spoken word – the voice of God whereby we are changed and renewed. Which word do you prefer, the written word or the spoken word? If you were to get a love note from your honey (a colloquialism for loving spouse), then how would you prefer to have the note delivered? Would you want a store-bought greeting card – or do you want to hear it as a whisper in your ear? Hum, I thought so. And so it is with your Lord and Savior; He loves you and wants to speak love and truth to you – as a whisper in your mind.

---

[18] Ibid, Behave, B.1, anastrophe (391) "a turning back." and Strong's: "to overturn; to return."

The Hebrew word '*dabar*' (1697) meaning "a word" is derived from '*dabar*' (1696) meaning, "to arrange, but used figuratively (of words) to speak." [19] Words can be arranged to say specific things, so it is imperative to understand the inherent meaning and the context in which they are communicated. Words can quite easily be taken out of context, misconstrued, misinterpreted, maligned, misapplied, and mistakenly misrepresented, and for this reason the Spirit was sent by Jesus… to guide us in all truth. Much is missed – when taken out of context.

Do you believe Christ still speaks to us today? OK, and do you believe Christ speaks a word to you as well? By now, I hope so, because the written word is not a substitute for the *rhema* (utterance) word that originates in *logos*.

All of us have received spiritual understanding by reading the Bible, but this premise is humanly flawed. "All scripture is God-breathed" (2 Tim. 3:16), it is given by inspiration of God; all scripture "words" were spoken by the Spirit to Spirit-directed men and any understanding that we have is by the illuminating work of the Holy Spirit within us who guides us into all truth. How can we profess to "know the Lord" if we have never had a personal experience or heard a personal life-giving word from Him? How else can you prove He exists? If you want to know the Lord, then I will also tell you to read your Bible, but words in books are not the source of spiritual life; the Spirit of God is! Jesus is the Life! The Spirit is life! Books do not impart life; words draw us into the knowledge of truth and life, just as the Law was written as our tutor to keep us under guard and to bring us to Christ (Gal. 3:23, 24); yet it is the Holy Spirit who brings understanding, so, if you want understanding, then start listening so as to hear what the Spirit is saying to you. "The Spirit is life" (Rom. 8:10; John 6:63). The kingdom of heaven produces life… and Jesus is the Life.

---

[19] Strong's Concordance.

Understanding by reading can only take you *to* the truth; spiritual understanding, as directed by the Holy Spirit, will lead you *into* the truth… and peace… and beyond!

"In the article on READ, Vine defines the word ANAGINOSKO as meaning "to know certainly, to know again, recognize." However, to "read" something does not mean you know certainly, nor again, nor that you recognize anything, nor that you know *upward* (another definition of ANA). It simply means you read it." [20]

Final Authority

One Sunday, I passed by a TV when the Spirit caused me to attentively hear a well-known Atlanta preacher's message about listening to God. He was telling this congregation and millions of TV viewers that the Bible is the final authority on God's word. I am not bashing this man's ministry, as I would also then be bashing an entire culture of Godly men who have been taught to think this way, but *Jesus is* "the Word of God" (Rev. 19:13), Jesus is the final authority as the Word and Jesus continues to speak to us today through "the Spirit of Jesus" (John 14:26; 15:26; 16:14, 15; Acts 16:6).

Jesus is the final authority on the word of God because He is – the Word of God. Amen!

And Jesus is still speaking to us today through the Holy Spirit. The Bible (as the written word of God) is not the final authority on the Word of God – Jesus is! Jesus will always be the final authority to make manifest the words of God and the will of God – in the church age – and the kingdom age that is upon us now."[21]

> "And Jesus came and spoke to them, saying, "All authority has been given to Me in heaven and on earth" (Matt. 28:18).

---

[20] Vine's Expository, introduction to the expanded Vine's, p. vi.
[21] Image, p. 61, book #2 in the Image Bearer series by the author.

This culture within the institutional church is one reason why the Holy Spirit has been minimized and restrained because they believe the works, spiritual gifts and utterances of the Holy Spirit have ceased since the scriptures were written and, therefore, the Bible is the final authority. "The completion of the Holy Scriptures has provided the churches **with all that is necessary** for individual and collective guidance, instruction and edification."[22] Oh really? Thus, we have elevated the written word (Bible) above Christ Himself who said, "I still have many things to say to you" (John 16:12) and we have also elevated the preacher and priest above the voice of the Spirit – who continues to inspire these men with spiritual understanding through words that proceed from their mind out of their mouths. Man takes the credit – while the Spirit is muzzled.

And it is for this reason this current church-age generation of teachers and preachers must pass away because they will not alter their opinion and doctrinal prejudice concerning the things of the Spirit, as though it might repudiate the authority of their message. So, they are content to invite revivalists to come and speak a 'fresh' word from the Lord for the faithful to draw nearer in intimacy with God… as if this was a new word being delivered to awaken complacent hearts and minds that have fallen asleep. Do we need revival – or do we need reformation? The issue is this: we need to listen! If the Spirit were to move now, the complacent church cannot hear nor will it understand the means, the manner, the messenger or the message of what the Spirit will speak regarding the kingdom of heaven that is at hand.

How unexpected. Jesus brought words of revival and healing into this world which His church has been called to manifest, but now the church itself needs revival… and reformation!

---

[22] Strong's Concordance, commentary on '*glossa*' (G1100), paragraph 4, as his general opinion and that shared by others as well on the Bible as the final authority – and that there is no continuation of spiritual gifts such as tongues after "apostolic times nor indeed in the later times of the apostles themselves."

Understanding is oftentimes rooted in a personal experience, as having had a definable moment, but spiritual understanding comes by way of the Spirit whereby "you know that you know that you fully understand." If this definable moment can only come to you by way of the written word, then ask the Author of the word to speak *rhema* understanding into your heart so that you fully comprehend what the Holy Spirit said to that person who was listening and writing His words. The Spirit wants to speak truth to us so that we can experience life in the Spirit through words from Christ!

Words that impart knowledge can only take you so far. Until you have experienced life in the word, then you have not known the Word of Life. The Holy Spirit is speaking to us in order that we may understand the "upward" ways of God. "That which is born of the flesh flesh is, but that which is born of the Spirit spirit is" (John 3:6). We must be born "anothen," anew from above, according to the Spirit before the divine conversation can begin.

A case in point: there are some who are reading these words, but they have no personal understanding of who the Father is – or who Jesus is. They may have never opened a Bible to read the word for themselves; their understanding about God is entirely based upon what "man" has spoken to them, as "Someone" who is full of wrath, vengeance and fury. Well, that is only partially true; these concepts about God were experienced by Israel because of one reason… they refused to listen to His voice. If you refuse to listen as well, then you know how that story plays out.

True sheep desire dialogue with the Shepherd, not shadows of a former operational pattern found in Judaism. The reason God judged Judaism so harshly – and rendered their covenant obsolete – is because they refused to listen, understand, and obey the message.

> "But this is what I commanded them, saying, 'Obey My voice, and I will be your God, and you shall be My people. And walk in all the ways that I have commanded you, that it may be well with you.'

> [24] Yet they did not obey or incline their ear, but followed the counsels *and* the dictates of their evil hearts, and went backward and not forward. [25] Since the day that your fathers came out of the land of Egypt until this day, I have even sent to you all My servants the prophets, daily rising up early and sending *them.* [26] Yet they did not obey Me or incline their ear, but stiffened their neck" (Jer. 7:23-26).

The Lord's message to you includes His purpose for everyone on planet earth: hear and obey My voice, have dominion over darkness (evil) and establish My kingdom of truth, light and love! But not everyone wants to do this, for many reasons, and thus for any of these reasons… they choose not to hear His voice.

The difference between *ginosko* knowing and *oida* understanding resides in a personal encounter resulting in a personal relationship with the Divine – and then leaning into Him so He can speak love notes in your ear. You are His beloved. Until that moment when you hear that word and you experience His presence, you will never fully understand just how greatly blessed and highly favored you really are to Jesus. You are His beloved.

During a class to hear God's voice, I encountered a certain young lady who had been told many negative things to her throughout her life – and she believed them. She was in bondage to the multitude of lies that had been spoken to her and it controlled the way she perceived herself as "not good enough." After several weeks of learning The Four Keys to hearing God's voice, the group was told to take a moment and ask Jesus what He thinks about us. After the class had ended, she and I were chatting at the back of the room when she indicated she "heard a word" but she wasn't sure if it was from God. When she said she heard the word "beloved," I was able to immediately give witness that it was a true word from Jesus. Not only did it line up with scripture, but it was also the word her soul needed to hear the most.

You are His beloved. Your soul desires to hear these words also! Until you hear Jesus call you by that name, words are only just words of encouragement, but when you hear His voice, these words become life-giving. The lover of your soul has just spoken words of life into the core of your being. You are *alive* – at last!

Hear To Believe

What, in your mind, is most important: "to hear" or "to understand and believe?" Most of the preachers that I have heard invariably and repetitively tell the assembly, "you gotta believe." But who will believe unless someone is sent to teach – and preach? This is exactly the conversation Paul is having with the church in Rome. Most preachers talk about the importance of preaching rather than the focus of Paul's message: hearing. So, let's take a look – and perhaps we will see "Who" was sent to teach Paul about the message.

"Who" We Listen To

The Apostle Paul asked a question in Romans 7:29, but He never answered it directly. "O wretched man that I have become. ***Who*** will deliver me from this body of death?" The Holy Spirit is Who – and Paul goes on to describe the Spirit-directed life in Chapter 8. Paul said he received all the words of his gospel by revelation – words spoken and revealed to him by the Lord through the Holy Spirit. He was taught by the Lord Himself! So, who will help you to hear the word of truth concerning your life in Christ? The Holy Spirit! Read the written word or listen to the spoken word, or both, but most of all – allow the Holy Spirit to speak *rhema* truth and understanding to you – which comes by way of God's revelation to you.

The main reason the world is still the way it is today – is because the institutional church has failed to mature according to the *rhema* word of Christ. The institutional church has decidedly closed its ears to prevent any possible hearing of God's voice through the Spirit, whereby it teaches only the written word of God, line by line, precept upon precept, but the Holy Spirit wants to teach us *logos* by *rhema* – to thoroughly understand and comprehend by hearing an utterance word from Christ. The Holy Spirit is an administrator, if you will, of Christ's church, for the building up of the body, unto the Head, who is Christ Jesus. It is the Holy Spirit who is bonding us to Jesus Christ. Unfortunately, the institutional church seems to be building the wrong kingdom upon the wrong hill – and is bonding saints to individual denominations entrenched in muted theology. The complacent church does not want to hear the voice of God, or hear a word of Christ or listen attentively to the Holy Spirit. This pulpit resounds only with the voice of man.

> "But the word of the Lord was to them, "Precept upon precept, precept upon precept, Line upon line, line upon line, Here a little, there a little," That they might go and fall backward, and be broken and snared and caught" (Isa. 28:13)

The word was conveyed, but they kept falling backward. What then, do you think will happen, when the church hears the sound of the Spirit and listens to the Word of God? Yes, indeed! Streams of living water flowing from the Spirit will flow through us; the *pneuma* wind of the Holy Spirit will blow where it wishes (John 3:8) and the God-breathed anointing will speak a life-giving word of Christ through every one of us – not just to us – but revelation through us!

The Spirit is like the wind, like a flowing river, and He is like a breath – always coming in and going out – flowing wherever He wishes and *desires* (*thelo* – 2309). The wind never stops, rivers never stop, breathing never stops – but the hardened heart of man can make the spirit-man spiritually deaf and impede the flow of the Spirit to just a mere remembrance regarding an ancient, former way of communing with God. Spiritual ambivalence to hearing His voice must stop! This is not who you are – and this is why we must remember who we are.

God is the same yesterday, today and forever. He wants to speak to you right now – at this very moment – so soften your heart to hear what the mind of the Spirit is saying to you.

> "For My people have committed two evils: They have forsaken Me, the fountain of living waters, and hewn themselves cisterns—broken cisterns that can hold no water" (Jer. 2:13).

The Lord intended all along to have two-way conversations with all of His children. When He appeared with them at the mountain, the Israelites refused to hear Him, so the Lord gave them the written word, as if this was their burden and chastisement for refusing to listen. And we know that "all are cursed who do not conform to (continue in) every letter of the law" (Deut. 27:26; Gal. 3:10).

> "What purpose then does the law serve? It was added because of transgressions, till the Seed [Jesus] should come to whom the promise was made; and it was appointed through angels by the hand of a mediator" (Gal. 3:19).

The Law was added because of transgressions – *after* – they refused to listen and obey. Jesus came to satisfy the requirements of the Law and to set us free from this obligation, *if* we are willing to hear His voice, and live our life according to the Spirit... *and* do what He says.

This is the emphasis of the books I write and the reason I write... and this is exactly the same message that Paul preached to the Jewish nation 2,000 years ago. Remember who you are – and do not follow deaf and blind institutional leaders. They (Jewish leaders) were entrenched in their religious traditions and broken cistern theology and would not believe the message concerning Christ; they refused to hear. Now, 2,000 years later, Christian leaders are repeating the same transgressions by Israel; they are refusing to listen to the voice of the Spirit, or be guided by the

Spirit, or live in the anointing of the Spirit. The church prefers human doctrines rather than the sound of God's voice!

> "But what does it say? "***The word is near you***, in your mouth and in your heart" (that is, the word of faith which we preach): ⁹ that if you confess with your mouth the Lord Jesus and believe in your heart that God has raised Him from the dead, you will be saved. ¹⁰ For with the heart one believes unto righteousness, and with the mouth confession is made unto salvation. ¹¹ For the Scripture says, "Whoever believes on Him will not be put to shame." ¹² For there is no distinction between Jew and Greek, for the same Lord over all is rich to all who call upon Him. ¹³ For "whoever ***calls*** on the name of the LORD shall be saved." ¹⁴ ***How then shall they call on Him in whom they have not believed? And how shall they believe in Him of whom they have not heard?*** *And how shall they hear without a preacher?* ⁵ And how shall they preach unless they are sent? As it is written: "How beautiful are the feet of those who preach the gospel of peace, who bring glad tidings of good things!'"
> ¹⁶ ***But they have not all obeyed the gospel***. For Isaiah says, "LORD, ***who has believed our report***?"
> ¹⁷ So then **faith comes by hearing**, and hearing through word[s] of Christ" (Rom. 10:8-17; "words of Christ" is the literal Greek)

Let's examine the message woven between these wonderful lines of scripture. The audience Paul is writing to are unbelieving Jews; his relatives, friends, countrymen – and fellow teachers of the Law in the traditions of his forefathers. Paul is writing this letter to the Romans, that is, the church meeting in Rome made of Jews and Gentiles. This section was written specifically to fellow Jews; his heart is aching for them to believe, but how will they hear and believe the message? It is vitally important to remember that Paul did not come to faith by such a letter, or written epistle or even the spoken words of a preacher. Paul spent 14 years in Damascus for to receive "his gospel" (Rom. 2:16; 16:25; 2 Tim. 2:8; Gal. 2:1) directly from the source – the Holy Spirit! He is not just writing a letter that later became a canon of scripture; he is writing one of the most pivotal letters in human history!

V.8 – "The word is near you" can be a reference to (Deut. 30:14). This word is *rhema* (the Hebrew cross-reference is 1697); it is the utterance, spoken word, tangible message of God *from* God, which Paul is using in contrast to *logos* that he mentioned in Romans 9:6, 9, "But it is not that the word of God (*logos*) has taken no effect"… "those who are the children of flesh, these *are not* the children of God" (v.8). The *rhema* is near you and has always been near you – and so, also, is God, but listening does not make you a child of God any more than being born in a particular denomination does; hearing the utterance and obeying it does! Children of flesh live according to the flesh; in contrast, the children of God live by the spirit according to the Spirit; they hear His *rhema* voice and then make a confident firm decision to be an obedient believer, follower and disciple. The *logos* (fully expressed truth of God) is being preached, but saving faith only happens when you listen intelligently, hear *rhema*, understand and then – obey!

V.13 – "For "whoever **calls** on the name of the LORD shall be saved'" is a reference to Joel 2:32. The Apostle Paul is leading them to faith using the written word of God (i.e. the Jewish book of faith, since there was no such thing as a New Testament yet to institute or to delineate from an Old Testament), so that they can hear the *rhema* utterance, spoken word of God. For the reader of the Bible today, these words are written, but in the day of Paul, these letters were typically read aloud. Regardless of whether these words are orated by the mouth or read with the eyes, these messages constitute the *rhema* word of God – and God gets all the credit (glory) because they are His words, not the words of man or the religious teachings of any denomination.

V.13 – "calls" is a very powerful and provocative word. This word "*epikaleomai*" (1941) means, "*to call upon* by way of adoration" [23] and is contrasted again with the conversation that Paul began in Chapter 9, verse 25, "*kaleo*" (2564) meaning, "to call by a name, to name, to bear a name; thus it suggests either vocation or destination."[24] Children of faith *call upon* their heavenly Father in reverent adoration as Daddy within the context of having a personal relationship with Him – and by communicating with Him, whereas children of flesh call out to Him as "a destination" with a name. Now do you see why it is important for us to see each individual word of scripture in order to comprehend the essence of the words (*logos* truth) that God is communicating to us? Are you speaking "at Him" as a word to be deposited in heaven's mailbox hoping that you get a response, or are we communicating *rhema* words with Him in loving, reverent adoration relationship with Him – and listening attentively to hear His reply?

V.14 – "How can you call on Him unless you believe… and how can you believe unless you have heard?" This is the line in the sand once again. The truth of the gospel is not about sending more messengers or preachers or evangelists or Bibles or whatnot; the truth of the gospel is "believing" what you heard and incorporating it into your heart so that it becomes – FAITH. We have made preaching and evangelizing the object of faith *rather* than hearing, and it has dulled our spiritual senses such that we no longer recognize the voice of the Holy Spirit. We read and listen, and then listen and read some more… without ever hearing. The enemy is thoroughly delighted when self-professing Christians read their Bible and listen to spiritual words without ever hearing the message of Christ that should produce fruit in abundance within their heart.

Paul is asking many rhetorical questions here and it seems he is using religious arguments that have been used over and over again within tradition-laden Judaism. Who? What? and How? …are

---

[23] Vine's Expository, CALL.
[24] IBID.

often followed by "buts" when people make excuses for refusing to hear and believe.

I have yet to read a commentary that has proposed what I am about to propose, so take it for what it's worth and judge it accordingly – according to the Spirit. It does not seem to me that Paul is asking the church in Rome to send and equip messengers of the gospel; rather, these appear to be rhetorical questions that are intended to lead the hearer into a deeper understanding of the truth residing within the message. Paul used the same literary style in v.7:29: "Who will deliver me from this body of death," as well as the four rhetorical "who" questions in v.8:31-35. Paul is repeatedly asking questions that the audience should know the answers to. Paul is leading and asking and leading again and asking again the same question until – eureka – the listener gets it and writes this truth on their heart… and they believe! "What then shall we say?" (v.9:14) "What then shall we say?" (v. 9:30). Paul is teeing up the Q&A with his typical logic-based crescendo style culminating in a word of truth in verse 17….

V.16 – "But they *have not* all obeyed the gospel. For Isaiah says, "LORD, who has *believed* our report?" Literally: "Who has *been persuaded to trust in* our report?" This is the line in the sand that separates the children of flesh from the children of God. "Who has *heard* – and believed?"

"Lord, who has believed our report? And to whom has the arm of the LORD been revealed" (Isa. 53:1). The word "report" is '*akoe*' (189) meaning, "a thing heard, the sense of hearing," so that **true spiritual hearing** *implies…* **understanding the message**. The Hebrew word "revealed" is *galah*-1540' and is similar to the Greek work '*apokalupto*-601' meaning, "to uncover, unveil."

V. 17 – "Then faith comes by hearing, and hearing by word(s) of Christ." The word hearing is '*akoe*' (189) meaning, "the sense of hearing" that results in hearing and understanding the message. It is not just the mere tangible hearing of the ears (by the organ), but the hearing of the message to produce intangible supernatural faith ('*akoe*' is the same word that is also used for 'message' and 'report'). The Apostle John used this same scripture (John 12:38) and Paul employed the word '*akoe*' again in his letter to the church in Thessalonica:

> "For this reason we also thank God without ceasing, because when you received the *word* of God which you *heard* (*akoe*) from us, you welcomed it not as the *word* of men, but as it is in truth, *the word of God*, which also effectively works in you who believe" (1 Thess. 2:13; i.e. the truth of the message is effectively working *in you* to believe!)

Hearing (*akoe* – hearing the message)[25] is associated with *logos* – the word of the message. This is the "word of the message" and "the word of hearing" that the apostles preached. All three "words" mentioned here are *logos*, not *rhema*.

We get *logos* (the message) by *rhema* (the hearing of utterances spoken by men or as spontaneous thoughts from God or His Spirit), but this is not as logos coming from men, but as ***all*** logos coming from God! And it is not the hearing that comes by way of the ears, but as "the hearing" with instrumentality of our soul and spirit – by the Spirit. This truth must become crystal clear in our mind, so read it again. The phrase "the word of God" quite literally is, hearing "word(s) of Christ" and is akin to Heb. 4:2 "the word of hearing – in which you heard."[26]

V.17 – "So then faith comes by hearing, and hearing by the *word* of God." (NKJV) The object word here is hearing – not faith; and the vehicle of 'hearing faith' is coming through *rhema* (spoken utterance) words spoken by Christ Himself – to you! You can read it or listen to it without having use of the eyes or ears because ***"hearing" is a spiritual dynamic as a work of grace by the Spirit within you "to hear and to believe" so as to "understand the***

---

[25] "Hearing, also denotes the thing heard, a message" Vine's Concordance, Message, 2.

[26] Ibid, word study for message, 2. akoe.

message" – of Christ. This verse is powerful on its own and needs no commentary – through which the Holy Spirit speaks to every believer who calls upon the name of the Lord in reverent adoration and worship – by hearing the voice of Jesus. Hear the word of the Lord! Listen to His voice! Jesus and Isaiah told us, "They will be ever hearing, but not hear" because spiritual hearing that produces faith is not done through physical auditory listening by the ears – it is done with the spiritual ears within us to transform the spiritual mind (the thought process that results in understanding the message) that brings revelation to the spirit-man within you!

V.18 – there is a change in the manner in which Paul continues the Q&A that follows this verse. "But I say, have they not heard?" and "But I say, did they [Israel] not know?" (v.19). Two more rhetorical "buts" follow in verses 20 and 21 for a people who did not want to hear His voice. "I say then" (v11:1) is a return by Paul to his impassioned plea for Israel to hear and know and understand and believe – by hearing words of Christ. Without faith in Christ by hearing His voice, whereby they make a profession of faith with the mouth and believe in their hearts – they cannot be saved. Paul is pleading fervently in this epistle for Israel to hear and believe, not with the hearing of the ears, but with the hearing of the spiritual mind as that element of the soul that conceives, thinks intelligently and believes the truth that leads to faith (being thoroughly persuaded and convinced).

There are many who will read these words and will not hear (receive) this message or hear the truth (believe the report) because they are blinded by anger, doubt, bitterness, resentment, believing the lies of the enemy, shallow teachings about Christ, the spirit of entitlement, woe-is-me excuses, and what have you. They want a God that makes them happy, but God's plan is not about making people happy! God is looking for people who delight in Him because they have the joy of the Lord within them – as a people who hear and reverently call upon (adore) His name, whereby, He is delighted to lovingly reply, "Draw near, My beloved."

Hear the truth – understand the message – and believe. It is not that our neighbors have not heard and it is not that Israel has not heard and it is not that the nations have not heard; the word has gone out – the Holy Spirit has made sure of this, so that we are "all without excuse," but "they" have not believed the report. Some have hardened their hearts which they themselves have hardened as the result of making a mental decision not to believe so as <u>not</u> to "hear" the truth. They don't want to hear. They are without excuse. We are all without excuse! The word has gone out and we have heard it – the Spirit has made sure of this – but some refuse to believe the message of Christ. O, how the heart of our loving Father grieves when the people who are called by His name reject His Son regardless of the excuse. God will forgive our sin, but He cannot forgive excuses.

Do you love Jesus? Do you really, really, love and adore Jesus?

Now, look at the Parable of the Sower from this same perspective and you will see that Jesus is teaching us that the soil is a metaphor for how we listen, hear, understand and appropriate truth in our heart that results in obedience. Truth is a precious pearl that must be buried deep within our heart for our faith in Christ to grow, mature and produce a fruitful harvest. Salvation is the byproduct of this obedience, not the reason of faith whereby we are saved.

"Hear, O Israel" – listen and obey. Hear, O church – believe and obey. "Who then, after hearing, disobeyed?"

Hear Him! Return, remember who He is, remember who you are – and be saved!

> It's all about Jesus – and God gets the glory!

A Failure To Communicate

Many of us can recall the phrase from the 1967 movie 'Cool Hand Luke' - "What we've got here is a failure to communicate." Seconds later, a gunshot ended the scene quite abruptly. We are not in a stand-off with God who is intent on punishing us for wrongdoing, as was the case with Luke (played by Paul Newman).

God really wants to communicate with us, talk to us, and share His thoughts with us – because He loves us.

> "For I know the thoughts that I think toward you, says the LORD, thoughts of peace and not of evil, to give you a future and a hope. ¹² Then you will call upon Me and go and pray to Me, and I will listen to you" (Jer. 29:11, 12).

Loving thoughts and loving words – that is how I would describe the ways of God toward man… as understandably loving. Until a person is ready to hear God's voice, He is patient and longsuffering with lovingkindness. "He knows that we are dust." God does not condemn you and neither does Jesus (John 3:17), but, unless we repent and convert (change our ways according to who we are), then the end is quite predictable; we have ushered our own death sentence into an eternal life of hellish torment. This is not what our loving Father desires for any of His children – earthly or heavenly. The Father wants fellowship with us – by communicating with us. We are His children, so open up your heart so that you can hear His voice.

Many of us are familiar with the Greek word "*koinonia*" (2842) as it pertains to Christians living in fellowship with one another, which means, "having a common (*koinos*) partnership, fellowship," but it also implies a "fellowship manifested in acts, the practical effects of fellowship with God, wrought by the Holy Spirit in the lives of believers as the outcome of faith (read Philemon 6)."[27]

God wants to fellowship with us and have a personal relationship with us – in the same manner as when He walked with Adam and Eve in the Garden. God communicated with man in the beginning – and He wants to do it again, today, with you. However, there are times when man is not able to commune with God – when the presence of sin gets between you and the presence of God; sin

---

[27] Vines Expository, communion, definition and example (b).

separates us from God's intent to fellowship with us – and to communicate with us.

The Greek word for communicate, quite predictably, is related to *koinonia*; it is *'koinoneo'* (2841) and "is used in two senses, (a) to have a share in, (b) ***to give a share to, go shares with***"[28] and to be a partaker of God's things. Most of us have never been taught to perceive God from this perspective, that God wants to "go shares with us," but this is precisely what our Father wants; He wants to partner with us! Before we can "go shares with" God and have a share in the things of God, we need to have "a share in" the Divine relationship with God that focuses on loving fellowship built upon trust and understanding. We need to focus all our attention and affection on Jesus Christ, for He alone is the Way, Truth and Life (John 14:6).

The Father wants "to give us a kingdom" (Luke 12:32), "to give us the keys of the kingdom" (Matt.16:19), to reward us, "to have a share in," "to share in the inheritance of Christ" (Eph. 1:11, 18; 5:5; Col. 1:12; 3:24) and "to put all things under our feet and His feet" (Psa. 8:6; Eph. 1:22). All things were delivered to Jesus by the Father (Matt. 11:27), dominion and authority were restored to Jesus Christ – and then Jesus gave His dominion to us prior to His ascension.

In order for us to fully embrace the wonderful things that God has planned for us, we must be able to hear His voice. (How do you think I am able to write these words to you at this moment? If you think that I am writing them with super-spiritual understanding of scripture, then I hate to disappoint you. It is not about how smart you are or if you have gifted speech… I have become one thing: an excellent listener. For me, understanding the truth has become simple: listen, hear, tune to flow, write it down, and then comprehend. The Lord gets all the credit, not me! I am just a gardener… who is listening.)

---

[28] Strong's Concordance.

However, we will never be able to fully comprehend this marvelous truth if we have resigned ourselves to think only of ourselves as "wretched sinners, worthless human beings, grasshoppers, and lowly slime that crawled out of the primordial cesspool of life." I was unable to know the truth about "who I am" until I finally heard His voice tell me "who I was." He called me by name – He called me "beloved."

That is why the first of these books was written. Regenesis is about remembering *who* we are. The Image Bearers series is about knowing– *why* and *what* to do – so we do those things which we are called to do – and this entire process begins by hearing His voice (Rom. 10:17). How will you know the truth unless someone tells you? Precisely! But it is not these written words or the preacher's spoken words whereby you will understand; hearing words of Christ comes by the Holy Spirit Himself who '*dianoigo*' *opens* your mind to the truth. These written words began as *rhema* words spoken to me when I heard them, but now they are becoming an *"expression leading to understanding"* to whomever is reading this, through an intermediary – this book; however, the Spirit wants to speak *rhema* to every one of us so that a personal relationship with Christ is established in us so that we can "have a share in" the wonderful things God has planned for us.

Hearing through a word of Christ can be interpreted several ways, but the end result is the same: Hear Him! Then do it! If the only way you will ever hear a word of Christ is by listening to the preacher, then listen – hear – understand – and then write it on your heart. If the only way you will ever hear a word of Christ is by reading the Scriptures, then read – hear – and then write it on your heart. If you hear a word of Christ and it comes as a spoken *rhema* word (voice of God) in your mind – then write it on your heart. If the only way that you will ever hear a word of Christ comes by any means, then pay attention, listen intelligently – hear – and then write them on the tablets of your heart. In other words... journal the truth so that you never forget the message which you believed... and be ready to run with this message (Hab. 2:2).

There are some who may have gotten the wrong impression about the message I have communicated through written words, so I want you to know confidently that – *I am not against the written word of God.* Nothing could be farther from the truth! That is how I came to the knowledge of the truth as a new Christian – and this, no less, by using the NIV. However, since it is the Holy Spirit that utters the word of Christ to all who will listen… "If you will hear," this book is about everyone knowing they can hear God's voice and what you can do to prepare yourself to hear – and obey.

Just Tell Us Plainly

This was a common phrase among the disciples, "Just tell us plainly" (John 16:29). And the religious leaders of that day were the same way,

> "Then the Jews surrounded Him and said to Him, "How long do You keep us in doubt? If You are the Christ, tell us plainly" (John 10:24).

"Jesus answered them, "I told you, and you do not believe. The works that I do in My Father's name, they bear witness of Me" (John 10:25).

It seems Jesus never told us anything plainly. He directs us to the door of truth and, then, He stops. God desires that we seek the truth in order to find it, but sometimes, He doesn't give us the answer right away. It is we who must open the door of truth to comprehend what we are entering into. He wants us to figure it out! Because, when we figure it out, two things happen: 1) we can never forget the Aha eureka moment when we truly understand the truth in our mind, and 2) Jesus is delighted when we finally comprehend the truth. Jesus is Lord of revelation.

The company of disciples had just asked Jesus if He was the Messiah, but Jesus did not tell them plainly; He simply said, "Who do you say that I am?" [29] I can only theorize how Jesus felt when Peter gave the answer that shook the world, "You are the Christ" (Matt. 16:16). Finally! Parable after parable of kingdom truth they did not understand, but this truth came in a way, not through knowing or understanding, but through hearing. "Jesus answered and said to him, "Blessed are you, Simon Bar-Jonah, for flesh and blood has not revealed this to you, but My Father who is in heaven" (v.17). So, how do you think the Father told Peter? He spoke a word in his mind at that exact moment – through the Spirit! Eureka!

The word "revealed" is *'apokalupto'* (601) meaning, "to uncover, unveil." It is used in the subjective sense in this verse – and also in John 12:38: "Lord, who has believed our report?
And to whom has the arm of the LORD been revealed" (Isa. 53:1). The word "report" is *'akoe'* (189) meaning, "a thing heard, the sense of hearing, so as to hear and understand *the message*."[30] "It is a combination of phrases which have been termed Hebraic as they express somewhat literally an Old Testament phraseology, e.g., "By hearing they shall hear." [31] This revelation of Messianic truth was revealed directly to the mind, in Peter's case, by the Spirit of the Father, for this was His good pleasure! Peter heard God's voice and made a bold proclamation.

God revealed, the Spirit spoke, Peter listened, and the Holy Spirit helped Peter figure it out. Peter came to the truth through understanding. It was not Peter's truth; it was God's truth for Peter to perceive and comprehend – and then… to believe and declare!

> "The secret things belong to the LORD our God, but those things which are *revealed* belong to us and to our children forever, that we may do all the words of this law" (Deut. 29:29).

---

[29] Jesus often answered questions with a question. As is most beneficial, a true teacher will lead a student to help them uncover or discover the truth on their own. This truth is rarely forgotten.
[30] Vines Concordance, word study on hear, hearing, AKOE (189).
[31] Ibid.

If you are searching for the truth and you want to know an answer, then ask the Spirit, "what does this mean?" God loves all His children passionately and He is no different than earthly fathers who desire their children grow up and mature in knowledge, wisdom and stature. The Father wants to reveal (uncover) truth to us so that we may attain "the full measure and stature of Christ" in us (Eph. 4:13).

Have you ever had a child come up to you with the question, "what do you think?" Of course we have, but what do you think is most important, knowing all truth (facts) – or being able to help them and guide them to think into truth (perceive and comprehend)? Likewise, God wants us to mature and come to the knowledge of the truth for one reason: so that we think it through, mature and bear spiritual fruit. We were created to be fruit bearers.

See What May Come

In addition to "telling us plainly," there is another aspect of God's lovingkindness and longsuffering that is revealed in His patience… "to see what may come of it."

> "And he said: "I will hide my face from them, *I will see what their end will be*, for they are a perverse generation, children in whom is no faith" (Deut. 32:20).

There are times when the Lord is going to test us to see which way (what path) we will choose – and He will give us a long leash in order to see what we will do. Think about your life as having two ways (or pathways) that are parallel to each other; one way is the predetermined and predestined will of God for your life (prescriptive) and the other way (permissive) is the result of many individual choices you have made. Free will allows us to walk along either path – and sometimes we can walk with one foot on each path "to see what may come of us," but in the end, there is only one path that leads to eternal life. There is only one Way; it is Jesus Christ!

> "I searched in my heart how to gratify my flesh with wine, while guiding my heart with wisdom, and how to lay hold on folly, till I might see what was good for the sons of men to do under heaven all the days of their lives" (Eccl. 2:3).

> "I will stand my watch and set myself on the rampart, and watch to see what He will say to me, *and what I will answer when I am corrected*" (Hab. 2:1).

> "I will counsel you with My eye upon you (Psa. 32:8).

> "However, when He, the Spirit of truth, has come, He will guide you into all truth (John 16:13).

The Lord will lead us and guide us in the way of truth and, then, keep His eye upon us to see what may come of it (our response to His guidance and leading). Now, the Spirit of truth was sent to guide us "while we are on the way" with play-by-play instructions by speaking the truth of God to us as we need it; however, it is up to us to walk in the way, so that we may be open to hearing, following Him, and acting upon His guidance.

Allow me to put the trial and testing of our faith into four steps that I have experienced:

1. See what may come of it
2. Test and see (to proof-test what we've learned so see if *we* know; if we comprehend)
3. To see what happens next (looking with vision for the next step)
4. Wait and see (to see if we will jump ahead on our own initiative ahead of the Spirit)

From an earthly perspective, it seems our faith-walk in the kingdom is backwards from real life (if there is such a thing). In life, we go to school or job training in order to learn stuff, and then we are given a test to see what we have learned. In the kingdom, we are given a test to see what we will do and which way we will go, whereby we learn by being trained in righteousness. When we seek God to search out the answer to the test, He is delighted to tell us and show us what we need to learn from the experience. He is not hiding the truth from us – He is withholding it for a short time to see what may come of it – and to see if we come to Him seeking the answer 'first' before charging ahead with our self-directed plans and ideas.

Eyes Of Our Heart

All my Christian life, I believed that I have "eyes of my heart." It took me quite a while to find this scripture (in the NKJV), which I eventually did; it is Paul's prayer to God regarding the Ephesians:

> "That the God of our Lord Jesus Christ, the Father of glory, may give to you the spirit of wisdom and revelation in the knowledge of Him, [18] the eyes of your understanding (*kardia/dianoia*) being enlightened; that you may know what is the hope of His calling, what are the riches of the glory of His inheritance in the saints, [19] and what *is* the exceeding greatness of His power toward us who believe, according to the working of His mighty power..." (Eph. 1:17-19).

The word "understanding" is *'kardia'* meaning, heart (English, cardiac), yet some manuscripts have *'dianoia'* which means understanding (a thinking through – of the mind). Understanding is associated with the heart (*kardia*) as well as the mind (*nous*); "He completely opened (*dianoigo*) their minds (*nous*) to thoroughly understand (*suniemi*) the Scriptures" (Luke 24:45). There are two camps of people in Christ; one believes understanding is from the heart and one believes understanding is from the mind. From a spirit-man perspective, both are correct, since the heart and mind are both elements of the soul. God will speak to both – yet even more so to the one that is open – and is willing and able to listen.

Our spirit-man is able to see, hear and understand spiritual truth when the Holy Spirit brings revelation (uncovered, unveiled words of truth) to us. And the Holy Spirit is still speaking, guiding, sanctifying and transforming us just as much now as He did for the early church. Our spirit-man has "eyes of our heart" as well as "ears of our mind," so we may perceive and discern spiritual things, and also so we may understand (*suniemi* – 4920 – thoroughly understand, a mental putting together) what the Spirit is saying to us. The Divine relationship is all about understanding what God is doing – and why!

> "So that you incline your ear to wisdom, and apply your heart to understanding" (Prov. 2:2).

We listen with our spiritual mind. Through the dual operation of seeing and hearing (heart and mind oneness), our spirit-man is able to perceive truth, understand it – and comprehend it (put it together)! This truth needs to be buried deep within the consciousness of our soul, which becomes like a pearl of great price; sell everything you have to possess this oneness of heart and mind, so as to completely understand, being thoroughly persuaded and convinced (in faith) that results in obedience (from listening intelligently).

The dual operation of understanding needs to occur in our mind – together with our heart.

> "Lest they should see with their eyes and hear with their ears,
> lest they should *understand* with their hearts and turn" (Matt. 13:15).

Some translators teach us that we understand with our heart, and this verse can be used to support the use of *"kardia"* for understanding (as in Eph. 1:18), but allow me to emphasize this scripture using a rigid linear interpretation.

> "Lest they should see with their eyes and hear with their ears, lest they should *understand* [*suniemi- a mental putting together*] with [to put together/in combination with] their hearts – and turn [convert, turn away and turn to]" (Matt. 13:15).

It seems the prophet Isaiah and Jesus both comprehended the problem. People need to hear the truth and assemble the understanding in their mind (comprehend), as well as build (or plant) understanding in their heart, in tandem **with** each other, as one spiritual operation within the combined function of the spiritual soul of man in order to create true conversion. The door of our mind must be open to understand the message being heard – and the door of our heart must be open to understand the conviction by the Spirit to '*oida*' *perceive* and thoroughly comprehend the truth of the message.

> "Eye has not seen, nor ear has heard, nor have entered into the heart of man, the things which God has prepared for those who love Him" (Isa. 64:4; 1 Cor. 2:9).

The thinker (the mind) – in union with the knower (the heart) – best describes: the conscience (*suneidesis*-4983) meaning: co-perception; with perfect knowing.[32]

> "I call to remembrance my song in the night; I meditate within my heart, and my spirit makes diligent search" (Psa. 77:6).

Jesus quoted the scripture from Isaiah 64:4 for two reasons:

1. As one way of telling us – He is the Messiah
2. The (spiritual) things of God must be put into the heart by the Spirit of God – they do not come by hearing or by

---

[32] Strong's Concordance.

> observation (Luke 17:20) but as revelation by Divine utterance

Apart from the new birth by the Spirit, we will be ever hearing but never understanding the things of God's kingdom. It is not enough for us to hear the words of the preacher, or to listen to the testimony of individuals, or to see firsthand witnessed accounts of miracles, signs and wonders. Unless the Holy Spirit brings revelation with understanding to our heart and mind through the hearing of His utterance (the small still voice within us), then how on earth are we ever going to understand and comprehend the incredibly wonderful things that God has already planned (predestined) for us.

> "But God has revealed them to us through His Spirit. For the Spirit searches all things, yes, the deep things of God. [11] For what man *knows* (*oida*) the things of a man except the spirit of the man which is in him? Even so no one *knows* (*oida*) the things of God except the Spirit of God. [12] Now we have received, not the spirit of the world, but the Spirit who is from God, that we might *know* (*oida*) the things that have been freely given to us by God. [13] These things we also speak, not in words which man's wisdom teaches but which the Holy Spirit teaches, comparing spiritual things with spiritual. [14] But the natural man does not receive the things of the Spirit of God, for they are foolishness to him; nor can he *know* (*ginosko*) them, because they are spiritually discerned. [15] But he who is spiritual judges all things, yet he himself is rightly judged by no one. [16] For "who has *known* (*ginosko*) the mind of the LORD that he may instruct Him?" **But we have the mind of Christ**" (1 Cor. 2:10-16).

God reveals spiritual things and spiritual truth through His Holy Spirit, not in terms that man's limited '*ginosko*' knowing or wisdom teaches or understands, but through words of instruction by the Spirit (revelation) to God-fearing men and women who earnestly desire: A) to be spiritually minded; B) to understand spiritual matters; C) to perceive the heavenly reality of God's heavenly kingdom that surrounds us even now; and D) to operate with the mind of Christ. In this conversion, we are given divine assistance to operate with the mind of the Spirit, who intercedes on our behalf (Rom. 8:27), that we may '*oida*' understand the deep things of God from a firsthand, personal, spiritually discernible perspective: from a heavenly perspective… with the mind of Christ!

> "For to be carnally minded is death, but to be spiritually minded is life and peace" (Rom. 8:6).

> "Now He who searches the hearts knows [*oida*] what the mind of the Spirit is, because He makes intercession for the saints according to the will of God" (Rom. 8:27).

This is a working of the Spirit by the Spirit Himself. Jesus sent the Spirit for this reason: to speak revelation to listening minds that want to understand kingdom truth – and live it! Apart from the Spirit, we can know nothing – and understand even less. Without the Spirit of God, there is not even a verifiable seal that authenticates that we are God's spiritual children. The words we profess are not enough; they must be believed as truth – and put into actionable lifeways.

Sounding religious doesn't count. Acting spiritual doesn't count either. Believing without understanding is foolish trickery of the heart. Understanding without having an intimate personal relationship with Christ in your heart is intellectual ascent that lacks the substance of true spirituality. We need to be converted – in oneness of heart and mind! Only the Holy Spirit can guide us into this truth. The Spirit, the Spirit, the Spirit!!! He is the Gatekeeper of the Door, that is, Jesus Christ, and Jesus is the only Door that leads to life eternal.

The Apostle Paul was very familiar with this concept when He told us that salvation comes from making a proclamation with your mouth – and this is performed in the tandem "withness" of heart and mind oneness to produce a believing witness (*pistis* faith) within us.

> "But what does it say? "The *word* [*rhema utterance*] is near you, in your mouth and in your heart" (that is, the word of faith which we preach): ⁹ that if you confess with your mouth the Lord Jesus and believe in your heart that God has raised Him from the dead, you will be saved. ¹⁰ For with the heart one believes unto righteousness, and with the mouth confession is made unto salvation. ¹¹ For the Scripture says, "Whoever believes on Him will not be put to shame." (Rom. 10:8-11).

Does the scripture say "by the mouth and with the heart," or "with the mouth and heart" as one faculty, or does it say "in your mouth and in your heart," as two independent faculties that are functioning in spiritual oneness? Indeed, as two independent faculties operating in oneness.

Thrice the word "believe" is used, which we oftentimes associate with faith (*pistis*); however, a similar word '*pisteuo*' is used here and by implication, means "to entrust, to commit one's trust, to be committed to" [33] that comes by being thoroughly persuaded and convinced. If conviction comes by way of the heart, then what is the energetic source where persuasion comes from? Is it not the mind of the Spirit that brings conviction to the heart? The mouth that produces words is merely the human element that communicates this sense of oneness of heart and mind that bubbles up from "within" the heart of the inner man.

---

[33] Strong's Concordance.

Ears Of Our Mind

I have never heard a teaching about the ears of our mind, so let's keep an open mind to hear what the spirit of this message is saying to us. Institutionalized religion tells us we cannot hear God's voice; that privilege is reserved only for priests and prophets. The second thing we are taught is, "don't trust your mind" because it was the rational mind that tripped over the threshold of offense that resulted in original sin in the Garden. So, then, if the mind is so corrupt, then why does the Spirit speak to us in our mind and spend so much time renewing our mind "through the washing of regeneration and renewing" to transform us into the image of Christ (Titus 3:5)? If the mind is so corrupt, then why does God say, "Come, let us reason together?"

Reasoning, in this regard, it not a negotiation with God that results in a compromise, but rather… a conversion wherein we return to our intellectual sensibilities whereby we come into agreement with Him to conform our thinking so as to align with His thoughts and His ways.

Jesus Himself taught us the importance of hearing and understanding with our mind, so consider these verses:

- "And hearing (191) they do not hear (191), nor do they *understand*" (Matt. 13:13; *suniemi – to put together mentally, to comprehend*)
- "The prophecy of Isaiah is fulfilled, which says, "Hearing (189) you **will** hear (191) and shall not *understand*'" (*suniemi*; v.14)
- "Lest they should understand (*suniemi – mentally comprehend*) **with** their hearts" (v.15)
- "Therefore, hear [the meaning of] the parable of the sower: When anyone hears the word of the kingdom, and does not understand (*suniemi*) it…" (v.18, 19)

The hearing with the mind is only partially responsible for understanding; the heart must also hear – and this is done **_together with_** the mind to produce '*oida*' understanding. The mystery of faith must be believed in oneness of heart and mind. If you do not believe in oneness of heart and mind, then what do you suspect may happen concerning the message? It is understood?

And there is another key element needed to comprehend what Jesus is telling us. The hearing of faith is not done by hearing. I know this sounds confusing and contradictory, but it is very essential to comprehend this aspect of the spiritual reality and the kingdom of God: it must be spiritually discerned as a spiritual work within you by the Holy Spirit. "Hearing you will hear and shall not understand" is because hearing does not come by use of the auditory ears to hear, nor does seeing and perceiving come by use of the eyes to see. You can hear the message with your ears, but the hearing of faith comes by listening to the small still voice that the Lord speaks within you as the hearing of truth 'by your spirit.' The initial hearing that results in saving faith is the result of the Holy Spirit's work within you to hear the spoken utterance of God – and to understand what was spoken as well. It begins with conviction, followed by comprehending the truth that results in understanding.

Understanding the nature of the spiritual reality cannot be comprehended by observation or audible hearing (attentive listening; 3907; Luke 17:20); ***it must be spiritually discerned***. The Israelites saw and heard (sensed) God on the mountain, but they did not want to hear and understand the words being spoken to them by God – and thus, they continued in disobedience and unbelief. Jesus appeared again to Israel and taught them the same message – again, but they did not want to listen and hear then either. And to this day they walk in rebellion and unbelief.

And now, it seems, the institutional church is doing the same exact thing Israel did; we follow the written word, but do not want to listen to the sound of His voice or the Voice of Truth.

God's kingdom is spiritual. You must be born anew by the Spirit in order to discern, perceive and understand the things of this spiritual reality (John 3:8).

In the Parable of the Sower, Jesus tells us some seed fell by the wayside, which is often interpreted as the hard-packed shoulder of the road or path, which is not necessarily wrong, per se, but if we consider how the truth "fell by the wayside" to imply "fell to one side and not the other," then we may see another aspect regarding how the seed of truth with understanding was not appropriated in tandem (together with) the heart and mind:

> "When anyone hears the word of the kingdom, and does not understand it [*suniemi* – mentally put together and assemble truth to produce understanding by the intellect], then the wicked one comes and snatches away [the truth, apart from understanding] what was sown in his heart" (Matt. 13:19).

Many of our salvation messages are very strong in moving the heart to understand the gospel because our hearts only need the conviction of our spirit by the Spirit (like the faith of a small child), but until the truth of the gospel is also assembled in our mind and we become a living testimony, the glad hearing of the good news within our heart doesn't stand a chance when the evil one comes to attack us with lies and deception in our mind; he will "snatch away" (*harpazo*)[34] "quickly harpoon" the truth that was sown in the heart *before* understanding has an opportunity to take root. The mind needs to be as thoroughly persuaded and convinced in the truth, perhaps even more so, than the conviction which so easily is accomplished and manifested within our heart. We feel this initial truth as conviction, but we need to assemble this truth in our mind in order to completely understand in

---

[34] Harpazo (726) to snatch or catch away; "this verb conveys the idea of force suddenly exercised" in this case, by the evil one, Satan; Vines, study on the word catch.

heart/mind oneness to produce a true turning that results in conversion.

So, it is within this context that we can understand and appropriate true saving faith as told to us by Jesus in the Parable of the Sower (Matthew 13).

> "There is a way[side] that seems right to a man, but its end is the way of death" (Prov. 14:12).

The Parable of the Sower is about seeing our heart as a field for faith to receive the seed of truth *and* grow understanding. There are four types of soil in our heart all the time and we need to understand truth as it comes to us as "understanding" from God.

In Regenesis, I taught about the four types of soil in our hearts whereby we are able to receive truth; we all have wayside, rocky, thorny overgrowth and fertile soil in our hearts, but now I want to talk about the seed as words of truth that produce four types of understanding – as being partnered together with understanding in our mind:

1. the seed *apart from* understanding
2. the seed *of limited* understanding
3. the seed *growing in* understanding (amidst adversity)
4. the seed *with* fruitful understanding

"The seed that was sown by the wayside"[35] is the casual response to the initial hearing of the gospel message with '*akoe*' – "by the sense of hearing you will hear," but because they do not, choose not, cannot, or refuse to understand the message, the deceiver quickly snatches the seed of truth from the listener's heart. People in this respect, even though they may have made a verbal profession of faith, flicked their wrist, been baptized and even attend church every Sunday… they have 'save-not faith without understanding.'

---

[35] "Wayside" is literally '*hodos*-3598' + '*para*-3844'; a road alongside of, beside, near or contrary to "the Way."

It is not what we say or do that determines our salvation – ***but what we hear and understand that results in obedience to the Lord***!!!

This is the seed of hearing which Paul talks about: "by the hearing '*akoe*' of faith" (Gal. 3:3, 5) as distinctly separate from the type of faith born under the law. This seed of faith is born of the Spirit, but unless the recipient wants to understand, and wants to go deeper in the love-trust relationship with Christ, then they can pretend to have salvation, but this is not saving faith. "The word of truth has gone out and the message has been proclaimed" (Rom. 10:18), but "by hearing they hear and shall not understand" because they choose not to understand.

"The seed sown on the rocky ground" is the more attentive listener who received the joyful good news of the gospel, but goes back to life as usual – according to the life they want to live. They received the truth joyfully, they accepted the word of truth into their heart, but the truth did not take root – the message was heard and received, but saving faith was never established according to the terms of faith in Jesus Christ! "It is no longer I who live but Christ in me" did not take root, and thus, they go back to building their kingdom on their terms. This response can be likened to a young child who has become self-aware and throws temper tantrums when they do not get their way because they think, erringly, that (whatever it is) exists for them. They have the seed of truth *with limited* understanding concerning the things of Christ, lacking the obedience that must result. This is often characterized by the phrase, "God and I have an understanding," assuming a hybrid gospel of Christ on their terms has any merit whatsoever, which is no gospel at all! If anyone wants to be saved, it is on Christ's terms alone; Jesus only – and Him crucified! If your faith of understanding is "most of you with some of Jesus," or "what I believe is my business" without any evidence of obedience, then you have deceived yourself – and quite possibly others as well.

"The seed that lands amidst overgrowth" is the first evidence of saving faith. The truth was received in the heart, it took root and has begun to grow up in the things of Christ; however, the cares of the world are growing up faster than faith and thus have quickly choked the truth of faith from producing the fruit of righteousness. The soil is right for spiritual growth and the seed is right for understanding, but the gospel truth is growing side-by-side and competing against the weeds of doubt, fear and unbelief. There is a very interesting word that Christ used to describe *"the growing up"* of the thorns around the seed; the word is *'anabaino'* and is the same word used in the scriptures to imply 'ascend,' as in, "Christ ascended into heaven." It is also the same word Christ used in the very next parable about the faith of a mustard seed that "grew up" *'anabaino'* into a mighty plant (Mark 4:32). There is much we can discern here by comparison. We have all been planted as seeds upon this planet where the kingdom of darkness resides, and we were sown with the expectation that we will not only grow to produce a harvest (of glory), but we must also grow up faster in the truth of faith than the weeds of doubt and unbelief that surround us. Let me encourage anyone who reads this message: if you can see yourself in this field, but you are struggling in the truth of faith… then you are living with salvation and are being saved through sanctification. Continue to ask, seek and knock to receive more truth. You have been… you are being… and you will be saved. Just continue to grow in truth (preferably faster than weeds) and endure. The pearl of great price (the truth of God's glory within us) has been planted within your soul, so keep on keeping on – and persevere! Remain faithful in the truth of faith, press in, go deeper, and you will be saved. God is merciful and He knows us according to the soil that He has given us, the grace He has given us, and the working of the Spirit within us. God knows what you are up against – so continue to endure, persevere – and continue growing in the truth of faith to have "the mind of Christ." The Lord can smite the brambles at any time, so rejoice in the brambles like Br. Rabbit in the bramble patch… your day of deliverance will come as long as you continue to grow up into Christ. Do not shrink, do not whither, do not doubt – continue to believe – remain steadfast and you will be saved!

"The seed on fertile soil" is the message of truth that has believed and overcome all things – amidst adversity – with understanding.

We may perceive this person as having been given special soil and a dispensational gift that came without any obstacles to the truth of faith, and for some it has (as a gift of grace), but we all know this is not typical living on planet earth being surrounded by darkness. This person has overcome adversity, doubt, despair, tribulation, fear, cares of this world, choking by brambles, and verily everything that has raised its hand against the knowledge of God and Christ Jesus. The message of the gospel is not about being born with perfect soil or hearing the perfect gospel message or worshipping in the perfect church being seated next to perfect parents and neighbors. Ha! The gospel of Jesus Christ is all about overcoming adversity – and the only way that I have known how to endure the painfulness of trials, tribulations, and wounding by fellow believers in scarlet letter rejection is to patiently wait upon the Lord – and to hear His words of compassion and comfort to ease our troubled soul. Truly – we are not getting out of "this world" alive, and it seems, there will be many challenges along the way. The flower that blossoms in adversity, or the seed that produces a meager harvest during a drought, are precious to our heavenly Father. Remember this: the grape does not enjoy the crushing, but how else is wine to be produced? This is the truth of faith that overcomes "all things" with understanding, which comes from hearing His voice and abiding in the truth in order to remain faithful long enough to produce a harvest. It requires obedience to the truth! Our days on this planet are very short, so seek to understand, seek a deeper personal relationship with Christ, seek out the deep well of living water, seek the living bread, in "all things" seek – and the Door of salvation will always be open for you.

Obedience without understanding – is nearly impossible!

Listen, hear, _understand_, and obey.

1. Listen for the truth – and receive it – as the hearing (the truth) of faith
2. Hear and believe the truth – *pistis* – being thoroughly persuaded and convinced

3. Hear and understand the truth – *akouo* – live like disciples and grow up in it
4. Hear and obey the truth – *shema* – and give God all the glory in it

Parables were spoken by Jesus to the multitudes, not to keep the people from knowing the mystery – they were spoken in such a way to stimulate questions resulting in a journey to inquire about and ascertain meaning with understanding. The disciples were just as confused as the people, but Jesus explained it plainly to them so that they would understand because they needed to understand right there and then. Why? Because disciples are active participants in a journey experience who follow a teacher to learn truth, but spectators attend to watch a good show or get a free meal without any intention to hear, understand, follow and obey.

Parables were told to us by Christ for several reasons:

- To cause questions to arise (*anabaino*) in our minds so that we are intrigued to seek and comprehend the truth that was hidden "for" us to find
- To draw diligent and earnest seekers into the ask, seek, knock journey to have an encounter experience resulting in true spiritual understanding
- To train our senses into spiritual sensibilities
- To guard the truth "from" people who may become careless with it

This is what Christ told the disciples in the Upper Room on the first day of His resurrection, "Why do (thoughts of) doubt arise (*anabaino*) in your heart?" (Luke 24:38). Over and over again the Lord Jesus is teaching us to understand, with heart and mind oneness, to search for, find and believe the truth of God by grace through faith.

What may be some of the reasons why people do not want to understand parables?

- They did not want to listen before (John 5:37)
- They do not thirst for truth (John 7:37)
- They have no interest to move the truth from the head to the heart
- They do not want to change how they think
- They have predetermined not to believe (John 10:23)

Truth is inconvenient because it requires a deliberate response one way or another

The parables have truth hidden within them, not because Jesus was hiding the truth from anyone, nor was He revealing it only to the disciples; the parables were spoken in mystery for one reason: to determine who is willing to seek understanding – and overcome all adversity in this journey to comprehend and thoroughly understand truth regarding the mysteries of God's kingdom. The truth was not hidden *from* us, but rather – the truth was hidden *for* us to find.

So, then, who are you? Are you a seeker and finder, or are you a passive participant who prefers to make excuses and blame brambles and other persons for your problems? Is this not the blame game that Adam and Eve played in the Garden? Now is the time for us to "grow up" in the truth of faith – and gain understanding in the mind *with* the heart!

> "It is the glory of God to conceal a matter, but the glory of kings is to search out a matter" (Prov. 25:2).

God hides truth because He delights in those who diligently search it out – and find it.

The Father is seeking worshippers who are earnestly seeking Him – in spirit and in truth (John 4:23, 24).

A Time For Understanding

The time has come for the church to teach more about understanding.[36] To tell conversion candidates that all one must do to be saved is "to confess with the mouth and believe in the heart and you will be saved" is exactly what the scriptures "do not" teach (Rom. 10:9); the fullness of conversion teaching is far more intricately woven and interconnected with thoughts of the mind that results in understanding, comprehension and obedience. We need the full gospel truth whereby the Holy Spirit convicts hearts as well as enlightens minds – thus allowing the Holy Spirit unrestricted access to sanctify our heart and mind – to understand the truth.

Many months after writing this chapter, I took a class to learn how the human brain operates. It is truly amazing how the brain receives messages and creates memories; this process is not linear, but iterative, like thoughts flowing in, then out, then in and out again to "build" memory. The human brain has a memory storage capacity of 3 million years worth of data, and while this factoid seems incredible, the next thing I learned literally blew my mind: the mind feels emotion and the heart has a mind.[37]

We often think of our soul as residing in the heart, so perhaps, in order to understand what I am about to say (or write, that is), we need to comprehend that we do not have a soul, but rather, we are a soul and that our inner man is "who" we really are; we are a living soul, and we living life in an earth suit from the inside out.

Some people have defined the soul as mind, will and emotion, but we will learn the soul is the mind and will, and our heart/spirit is the emotion and feeling aspect of our being.[38] The parts of our brain that correspond with each of these soul functions are as follows:

---

[36] Read book #4 in the Image Bearer series: "Understand" by the author.
[37] "Who Switched Off My Brain" by Dr. Caroline Leaf, copyright 2007.
[38] Read "Commission" chapter 1.

- Will – our free will is actually a physical structure (component) in the Corpus Callosum
- Mind (or intellect) – is the Corpus Callosum (our thinker)

Since we were created to operate in mind and heart (soul and spirit) oneness, the brain was designed with the ability to feel emotion (in the Hypothalamus) and the heart has about 40,000 neurons to stay in constant 'thinking' communication with your brain. This redundancy was given to us by our Creator to help us maintain constant contact with Him (and He with us) should one faculty become compromised.

All external information must initially pass through a "door" in your mind, so, where do you think the door is that Jesus tells us through which we must "enter in" for eternal life? Personally, I have concluded this door is in our heart – and has always been there (John 10:9). It is the spiritual "lifeway and manner" through which the Lord reveals Himself to us without irrational thoughts or deceptive feelings from getting in the way.

We have two doorways that lead to faith in Christ – one in our heart and one in our mind, but there is only one Door, which is Jesus Christ. The door that leads to Christ has a Doorman, a porter or gatekeeper if you will, and this is the Holy Spirit, who helps us "to guard our hearts and minds in Christ Jesus" (John 10:3; Phil. 4:7) and He "will establish you (in true faith) and guard you from the evil one" (2 Thess. 3:3). God does not wish us to remain ignorant any longer. God wants us to walk in the truth.

> "This I say, therefore, and testify in the Lord, that you should no longer walk as the rest of the Gentiles walk, in the futility of their ***mind***, [18] having their understanding (1271) darkened, being alienated from the life of God, because of the ***ignorance*** that is in them, because of the blindness of their heart; [19] who, being past feeling, have given themselves over to lewdness, to work all

uncleanness with greediness. [20] But you have not so *learned* Christ" (Eph. 4:17-20).

In all these meditations to perceive and thoroughly comprehend what the soul is and where it is located, I have determined this: we are a soul. Our soul is who we are (our inner being; who we are as seen by God) and it permeates the very core, identity and entirety of our life as a spiritual being, as well as our heavenly substance dwelling in human tents called bodies. Our soul is neither in our physical heart or brain; our soul is the spiritual equivalent of heart and mind that are in constant communication to understand and comprehend all things. One may be weak or broken, or the other inoperable, but this I have learned: the Lord created us with redundancy, with dual operating systems in case one should become compromised or irreparably damaged. Our soul is who we are – and we desperately need the fullness of heart and mind communication, cooperation and coordination so that we may experience a celebration of truth with understanding within our soul as it receives revelation so that we can do one thing: magnify the Lord with our soul – and give glory unto Him!

Truly, I tell you, we have been wonderfully made and created. Regarding atheists, it is hard to comprehend having two doorways and, thus, rationally and intentionally choosing to close just one of them; and to evolutionists, it is hard to justify a theory that ignores the existence of free will, when it is a tangible, physical element of the mind (why would mankind evolve in such a manner is a mystery, and even if we could, where would any organism get this idea from).

Below is a diagram of the soul that many of you saw in my first book: Regenesis. The more information I learn about the mystery of who we are, as a living soul that is being sanctified, the more convinced I am that this diagram was given to me by way of the Spirit with understanding.

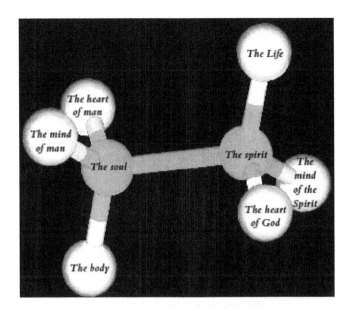

Jesus knows we have natural ears, but Jesus was always teaching us to comprehend the spiritual reality that surrounds us – as well as heaven's eternal reality within us.

> "So He said to them, "How is it you do not understand?" (Mark 8:21; also see Matt. 15:17; 16:9, 11; Mark 4:13; 7:18; 8:17; John 12:16).

> "Why do you not understand My speech? Because you are not able to listen to My word" (John 8:43).

Hardened Hearts

I'll tell you the main reason why we do not hear spiritual truth with our mind: because our hearts are hardened. Before our mind can hear God's truth – and understand truth, we need to come to the throne of grace with a soft heart that is able to *receive* the truth (which we will discuss in detail soon).

> "But Jesus, being aware of it, said to them, "Why do you reason because you have no bread? Do you

> not yet perceive nor understand? Is your heart still hardened? (Mark 8:17)

Hardened hearts will prevent us from hearing God's voice in our mind – and limit our ability to spiritually understand. Read it in reverse order: hardened hearts, will not understand, will reason futilely in the mind. Jesus told us we are not able to understand "His speech" because we are "not able to listen to (hear) His voice" (John 8:43). We need to soften our heart and surrender our will in order to open our mind to the reality of truth that resides in Jesus – in all of its myriad diversity and manifold wisdom that is *Logos* – the truth of God revealed in Christ!

Consider these scriptures to help see the connection between the mind and heart:

> "As for you, my son Solomon, know the God of your father, and serve Him with a loyal heart and with a willing mind; for the Lord searches all hearts and understands all the intent of the thoughts. If you seek Him, He will be found by you; but if you forsake Him, He will cast you off forever" (1 Chron. 28:9).

> "And God gave Solomon wisdom and exceedingly great understanding, and largeness of heart like the sand on the seashore" (1 Kings 4:29).

> "Who has put wisdom in the mind? Or who has given understanding to the heart? (Job 38:36).

> "So that you incline your ear to wisdom, and apply your heart to understanding" (Prov. 2:2; if the concept of "eyes of the heart" hangs on Eph. 1:18, then this scripture codifies the "ears of our mind").

> "For the hearts of this people have grown dull. Their ears are hard of hearing, and their eyes they have closed, lest they should see with their eyes and

> hear with their ears, lest they should understand with their hearts and turn, so that I should heal them" (Matt. 13:15).

> "When anyone hears the word of the kingdom, and does not *understand* it (4920 – *suniemi,* to put together mentally, to comprehend), then the wicked one comes and snatches away what was sown in his heart. This is he who received seed by the wayside" (Matt. 13:19).

> "... having their understanding (1271, see below) darkened, being alienated from the life of God, **because of the ignorance** that is in them, because of the blindness of their heart" (Eph. 4:18).

And again,

> Jesus said, "You shall love the Lord with all your heart, with all your soul, and with all your **mind**" (1271 "*dianoia*" – completeness of understanding, fully comprehending, meditative, deep thought[39]; Matt. 22:37; Mark 12:30; Luke 10:27).

> "I will put My laws in their **mind** (1271) and write them on their hearts; and I will be their God, and they shall be My people" (Heb. 10:8; Jer. 31:33).

And finally...

> "And to love Him with all the heart, with all the "*dianoia*" (understanding/mind) [1271 – *a thinking through, deep thoughts, meditation ,reflection*[40]], with all the soul [*the combined submission of the heart and mind in one accord*], and with all the

---

[39] A compilation of definition terms from Strong's and Vine's.
[40] IBID

> strength [*the yielded will and surrender of earthly desires*], and to love one's neighbor as oneself, is more than all the whole burnt offerings and sacrifices." (Mark 12:33; italics by author).

Results in this…

> "And the peace of God, which surpasses all understanding, will guard your hearts and *minds* ["*noema*" (3540) – perception, the intellect] through Christ Jesus" (Phil. 4:7).

If you were to take a guess which Greek word is used for understanding (above), would you choose *suniemi* (a mental putting together), *oida* (complete understanding), *nous* (reflective consciousness) or *dianoia* (a deep thinking through)? Take a moment to consider your choice.[41]

This may be an oversimplification, but if you want peace (or if the world wants peace), then you have to seek Jesus, who is the Price of Peace, and you must love Him with the totality of who you are (soul, spirit and body) and also surrender the elements of your 'self of soul' to Him (your heart and mind). Let the ears of your mind (intellect) be open so as to instruct the eyes of your heart to fully comprehend, perceive and understand how great the Father's love is toward us – even as we commission our soul (in heart and mind oneness) to love Jesus.

How, you may ask, can anyone attain this level of truth and understanding? The cost is simple: all it costs is everything you

---

[41] If you guessed *nous*, then you are more perceptive then I was. 'Nous' (3563) the intellect, i.e. the mind, seat of reflective consciousness, comprising the faculties of perception and understanding, and those of feeling, judging and determining[41] (Luke 24:45; Rom. 1:28; 14:5; 1 Cor. 14:14, 15 (twice), 19; Eph. 4:17; Phil. 4:7; Col. 2:18; 1 Tim. 6:5; 2 Tim. 3:8; Titus 1:15; Rev. 3:18; 19:7). Having been born anew, "this new nature belongs to every believer by reason of the new birth (Rom. 7:23, 25)." Strong's Concordance.

have. Become a disciple of Jesus... and enter into oneness with Him.

Reasons why we cannot hear – or understand

Listening is not a discipline for the natural ears to hear, but rather, a spiritual determination made by our soul (mind) to listen attentively – and listen intelligently.

1. Half-hearted listeners desiring to go their own way... should not expect to hear anything. Listeners desiring to hear – and walk in the way of Christ – will hear.
2. Sin creates a wall of separation between listeners and the Lord – and obstructs our ability to hear. Blatant and unrepentant sin will make hearing next to impossible. *You must remove the roadblock of disobedience in your mind that prevents you from hearing.*
3. Unforgiveness is one of the main obstacles preventing us from hearing His voice.
4. Unbelief is a refusal to understand, even though the message is heard.
5. Predetermined unbelief (to hear but never intending to believe) is "double-minded" and unstable thinking with wrong motives – by asking God to hear from Him, but never intending to alter your position in unbelief.
6. Rebellion is a determination sinners have made to never hear, obey or walk in the way.
7. Iniquity is the adoption of a lifestyle that is inherently opposed to the kingdom of God, and persons living in iniquity can only hear through a radical work of grace by the Spirit.
8. Wayside believers walking along a similar way (religion) that appears true, but is not, will hear the message, but will not understand because it is inconsistent with "their" way.
9. Hardened hearts are the primary reason why people cannot hear or understand (which will be explained)

Another Reason

There is "another" reason why they do not know nor do they understand…

> "They do not know nor understand; For He has shut their eyes, so that they cannot see, and their hearts, so that they cannot understand" (Isa. 44:18).

> "But they do not know the thoughts of the Lord, nor do they understand His counsel; for He will gather them like sheaves to the threshing floor" (Micah 4:12).

The Lord wants us to know His thoughts!!! He encourages us to seek Him, find Him, to know Him and to understand His thoughts and ways because He does not want to gather us like chaff destined for the fire. He wants wheat! How can God accuse us of wrong-doing in this regard? Indeed, He cannot, which is why Jesus came to teach us and show us the way to the Father. If we choose not to listen to Jesus or to understand, then that is our choice – and ours alone.

Consider the conversation that Jesus had with two angelic beings concerning Abraham: "Shall I hide from Abraham what I am doing…" (Gen. 18:17-23). Jesus can hear our thoughts, as He did Sarah's, but the only way Abraham could have recorded the thought-language of God in this section is if God "lets us hear His thoughts." [42] Ponder this truth.

"My thoughts are not your thoughts" is ***not*** a boundary line that the mind of man cannot and must not cross. On the contrary, it is an open invitation! God wants us to know His thoughts and to walk in His ways, which is why He sent Jesus to show us how to live, as intelligent, thinking, deliberate, understanding souls living in harmony with the Master of their soul; and "We have the mind of Christ." God wants us to hear His voice and learn from Him. We

---

[42] Notes from the NKJV Study Bible, Gen. 18:17.

are His delight – and I am absolutely convinced that He will tell you this. You are His beloved and you are His delight – but your heart must be softened enough for the ears of your mind to hear.

> ***"I want to know the thoughts of God – all the rest are details."*** – Albert Einstein

The Parable of the Sower is a monumental pivot point in Jesus' earthly ministry (Matt. 13:1-23). Prior to this, Jesus was teaching kingdom principles, but now He is communicating kingdom of heaven truth in parables. The people are amazed by these teachings – and perplexed – because they do not know what they mean because their hearts are hard. Even the disciples were confounded by their meaning, so they asked Jesus to explain. Jesus said the purpose of the parables is to communicate the mysteries of the kingdom of heaven. "To know" the mystery is the word '*ginosko*' with the idea of gaining and progressing in knowledge.

"For whoever has [knowing], more [understanding] will be given" (v.11). "Who" is giving the knowledge? "Who" will provide understanding? Knowledge and understanding are being revealed to man through revelation (*rhema* utterances) by the Holy Spirit, but understanding can be taken away (or withheld) as well. What could cause this?

Then Jesus said, "Therefore I speak to them in parables, because seeing they do not see, and hearing (191) they do not hear (191), nor do they understand" (Matt. 13:13). The word "hearing" is '*akouo*' meaning "to hear, listening" – but the operative word here is "understand." They are hearing (listening with the sense of sound), but they do not spiritually hear, nor do they spiritually *understand* (4920 – *suniemi,* to put together mentally, to comprehend, understand).

Why can't they understand? The Lord Jesus answered this question for us 2,000 years ago when He gave the answer to Isaiah (Isa. 6:9, 10; Matt. 13:14): their hearts are hardened and stupefied!

- "Hearing (189) you will hear (191) and shall not *understand* (4920 - *suniemi*),
- And seeing you will see and not *perceive* (1492 – *oida*: completely comprehend);
- ¹⁵ For the hearts of this people have *grown dull* (3975 – *pachuno*: dull, waxed gross, to thicken, to fatten, stupefy or render callous; with the idea of being fixed, "pegged" like a pitched tent); "For this people's heart is waxed gross" (KJV)
- Their ears (of their mind) are *hard* (917 – *bareos*: heavily, weighed down, burdened) of *hearing* (191 – conveying the sense of having heard many religious sounding, weighty words that have become weary, burdensome); "and their ears are dull of hearing" (KJV)
- And their eyes (of their heart) they have closed," (Matt. 13:14, 15).

The first time Jesus uses the word "hearing" in verse 13, is '*akouo*' (191) - to hear with the idea of understanding, but when He quotes Isaiah (v.14), the word for "hearing" changes to '*akoe*' (189) meaning, "the message." This is extremely important for saints who want to hear His voice and follow Him. So, let's compare and contrast these verses from Jesus' perspective:

- V.13 – you are listening to Me and you hear *akouo* My sounds, but you do not hear or understand *akoe* My message because you do not want to understand; you are choosing to stand in your own way and will not believe the message
- V.14 – you are hearing the message *akoe* with an interest to understand, and you will hear *akouo* with the sense of hearing, but you shall not understand because you have many burdensome beliefs that have hardened your hearts and you are unable to believe the *report* (*akoe* – *message*)

By the hearing of the natural ears they will hear, *but* they will not understand – because the hearing of spiritual messages that results in understanding does not happen by means of the human ears, but happens in a spiritually awakened mind by means of the Holy Spirit. If you are not willing to hear, then you remain stupefied and you are not ready to hear – and the Holy Spirit knows if you are ready – or not. It is the spiritual mind that is able, having been thoroughly persuaded and convinced... to hear the message and understand it!

When we apply these word definitions to the Parable of the Sower and our field of faith, now it all begins to make sense: we must hear it, understand it and implement it – *an actionable response by us is required.* And next, Jesus tells us how to reasonably apply these apparently conflicting scriptures:

> "Lest they should understand *with* their hearts and turn, so that I should heal them" (v.15)

Jesus wants us to understand in our mind (4920 – *suniemi*, to put together mentally, understand, comprehend) *with* our hearts (*kardia*) and turn. We are to understand truth in our mind – and align our heart with the message we believe.

The heart is the chief organ in the body and represents "the entire mental and moral activity, both the rational and emotional elements"[43] of man. Ok, this concept of heart we may know and readily accept, and Jesus told us we are to turn, but turn where, turn why and turn how? Herein is the keystone of faith: be converted!

The word translated "turn" is *'epistrepho'* (1994) and implies the idea of "twisting, to turn quite around or reverse" [44] in order to turn away from one thing and to turn around (twist yourself) toward something else, namely, to focus on Jesus Christ. The Apostle Paul uses an identical word *'epistrophe'* (1995) in Acts 15:3 within

---

[43] Strong's Concordance, word study for heart (2588) kardia.
[44] Ibid, word study for convert.

the context of having a revolution (conversion) of the Gentiles unto faith in Jesus Christ.

Hearing words of truth – and understanding the message – will make us more intelligent, though that is well and good also, yet hearing <u>*with*</u> understanding is intended to produce a revolution in our mind. Jesus is the greatest revolutionary in this world and, through faith in Him, the Spirit will transform and renew our mind – and then use His converted ones to revolutionize this world from darkness to light!

We are here to hear the message of truth – completely comprehend the message – be converted to the truth – and then convert the world with this revolutionary truth.

The Good News – is Revolutionary!

We are here to hear – and also – we are here to usher in a regime change from the kingdom of darkness and death… to the kingdom of light and life!

In this same passage, Jesus is using targeted words to convey two messages: to understand and turn – and comprehending that He is the Christ. The hearing, the perceiving and the seeing, which Jesus talks about in verse 16, serves as a direct link to those religious leaders around Him who want to know who Jesus is, and Jesus is telling them with scripture, but they do not '*suniemi*' comprehend it – or – perhaps they are choosing not to.

> "For since the beginning of the world
> *Men* have not heard nor perceived by the ear,
> Nor has the eye seen any God besides You,
> Who acts for the one who waits for Him" (Isa. 64:4)

Focus on Jesus – and hear what He says. Faith is not a one-time hearing event, but a continuous present perfect way of living with hearts prepared to hear – continuously turning to hear and focus on the Voice of Truth – and responding obediently.

By now, if this teaching has not waxed gross on some people or become a heavy weight to understand by scrutinizing and examining each little jot and tittle of scripture's words, then perhaps this is why we need to believe… as little children.

There is a past history, which we cannot understand apart from hearing; and there is a current history, which we cannot understand apart from hearing; and a time is coming soon that will be impossible to understand – unless we can hear! The point is simply this: if you are not listening and following with the entirety of self by being attentive to the Holy Spirit's prompting, then what is the whole point of faith and obedience if it is your will that you are implementing?

We must *turn away* from our way, our truth and our life – in order to *turn toward* His way, His truth, and His life. Oftentimes, we think we completely comprehend what this means, by understanding the meaning of faith and conversion, yet somehow, we go back to being "the governor" of our life – and the Spirit who comes alongside to guide us – grieves.

Jesus spoke using imagery to guide Spirit-directed learning, because apart from the Spirit, we can know nothing, nor can we discern spiritual truth apart from the Spirit. If you are not actively seeking the truth and looking intently and listening attentively, then you will miss all the clues to understand and comprehend – and be converted.

> "Assuredly I say to you, unless you are *converted* (1994) and become as little children, you will by ***no means*** enter the kingdom of heaven" (Matt. 13:15).

We must be converted (completely turned around as a result of hearing His voice) and **_we must become something new_** (as entirely different from what we currently are or were). We must be converted and become a new creation and become changed into something born anew, from above. This is not the mental assembling or putting together many words of wisdom, but rather, becoming sensitive to the simplicity of the gospel, to hear the voice of Jesus that is calling out to you, and to open the door of faith – like little children – who lovingly respond as when a parent calls them by name. Little children don't have agendas (or at least they shouldn't); they spend most of their time being delighted in the moment of playful joy to encounter new experiences and friends.

It is not enough to hear and believe; we must continue to hear if we want to understand and comprehend all truth – especially the age to come! This is the simplicity of faith that comes by the simplicity of hearing His small, still voice within us, but unfortunately, we burden ourselves with the weightiness of many teachings and institutionalized doctrines that enslave us once again to man's interpretation of what God is saying to us. When this happens, the results are often quite predictable, but when we turn, we will be healed!

> "Make the heart of this people dull, and their ears heavy, and shut their eyes; lest they see with their eyes, and hear with their ears, and understand with their heart, and return and be healed" (Isa. 6:10; Acts 28:27).

This seemingly scathing critique is actually very good news! Even if we have been converted (turned once), but then decided to go our own way, we can *return* once again – and be healed. We do not need to be converted again because we are still a new creation with a new heart and a new spirit, but now we need to *return* to our former way of walking in His way, the path of Christ. This beginning again happens when we hear with our spiritual ears (mind) and understand with our spiritual heart as the combined operation of our soul in converted oneness to follow Jesus only – and hear Him! But, if we do not return, then we have abandoned the only way whereby we are saved, having walked out of the very Hand that promised to protect us (John 10:27-29).

> "Now Moses called all Israel and said to them: "You have seen all that the LORD did before your eyes in the land of Egypt, to Pharaoh and to all his

> servants and to all his land— ³ the great trials which your eyes have seen, the signs, and those great wonders. ⁴ *Yet the LORD has **not** given you a heart to perceive and eyes to see and ears to hear, to this very day.* ⁵ And I have led you forty years in the wilderness" (Deut. 29:2-5).

This passage of scripture is for the people of Israel, who had seen the Lord's manifest presence upon the mountain and experienced the sound of His rumblings, but they ***refused*** His invitation to hear, draw near and obey the Lord's voice at the mountain; and thus, as an example, their rebellious hearts became hardened. This message was also intended for the disciples, whose hearts were not yet fully yielded (Mark 8:17; 16:14). Looking and seeing are not references to eyes and ears; they are metaphors for the heart and mind (the elements of our soul). If the mind has become weighed down and heavily burdened with your own thoughts and your own ways and the weighty cares of this life, then one thing will happen: you will harden your heart to become spiritually deaf. What, then, do you think happens if you continue to do this procedure hundreds of times every day of every week for years and years? Your heart gets closed.

> "Oh, that My people would listen to Me, that Israel would walk in My ways" (Psa. 81:13).

God wants us to know, understand and perceive kingdom-of-heaven truth. He does not want it to be a mystery; in fact, He wants to tell us *all* about it – and He wants to reveal it to you – but we must be able to hear Him. If you think God has shut your ears and your eyes so that you cannot understand or hear His voice, then check the condition of your heart. God did not close your heart, you did – which is the result of the self-directed will of the mind.[45]

---

[45] The Lord hardened the heart of Pharaoh (Ex. 4:21) and also the heart of the Egyptians for one purpose: to demonstrate to them that "I am the Lord" (Ex. 14:4).

There is a popular song in the church today; it is: "Open the eyes of my heart, Lord." In light of this teaching, the only person that can open the eyes of your heart – is you.[46] God will pursue us, chase after us, and circumstances and events that create opportunities for us to seek Him, but ultimately, the choice is yours. I pray that we will open the ears of our mind to this truth and begin the journey of revival that is located just 18 inches away.

God has been saying all along, "Come, let us reason together" (Isa. 1:18). As I mentioned earlier, this is not the reasoning that initiates a debate that results in a compromise; on the contrary, it results in an agreement – with you completely agreeing with the sovereignty of God – on His terms – with the Spirit helping you to understand what is happening.

Nebuchadnezzar lost his reasoning, but it returned to Him when he lifted his eyes to heaven and declared that God alone rules and reigns in the kingdom of men – and he acknowledged God's sovereignty and Lordship over his life. Obstinate, stiff-necked, hard-hearted and debased people who have lost their reasoning can only have their reasoning and soundness of mind healed (returned) in this manner: a choice must be made where there is no standing in between two ways. Furthermore (now get this), the Spirit wants to do something absolutely marvelous and more glorious than that: He wants to give us Spirit-anointed reasoning. There is only one thing that is separating us from this reality and a return to reason:

Hardened Hearts, Part II

This teaching is not about knowing how your heart got hardened, per se, it is about recognizing that your heart is hard, and perhaps closed, which prevents you from hearing God's voice. There are various reasons why we produce a hardened heart:

---

[46] The Lord did open the heart of Lydia (Acts 16:14). The word 'open' is *dianoigo* – thoroughly, completely open.

1. Sovereignty – like Nebuchadnezzar, we must acknowledge the sovereignty of God and declare His Preeminence. Until you declare Jesus is Lord, completely Lord, Master and King of your life, then you heart is not even turned toward Him is a positional manner, let alone a relational manner.
2. Forgiveness – if we have an impenitent heart, then God cannot forgive us until we first ask for His forgiveness – and then we are commanded to forgive one another (Matt. 6:14, 15; Matt. 18:35; Mark 11:25, 26; Rom. 2:5). Forgiveness opens the door of our heart to the presence of the Divine.
3. Hardness – comes from believing the lies of the enemy and, thereby, a reluctance to accept the truth of God when it is presented to you. The disciples also had hardened hearts, even though they walked with Jesus and observed all His signs and miracles.

We construct one kingdom or another in our heart based upon the thoughts we conceive and assemble in our mind. Our mind governs the "kingdom-building program" for our heart, and then the heart creates conditions resulting in life applications we call faith, character, and self-determination. Let me put this another way… the heart releases understanding that was originally put there by the thoughts of the mind. And God does the same thing:

> "I will put My law in their mind and write it on their heart" (Jer. 31:33).

This is the process whereby the heart receives truth and understanding – from the mind – and then releases it back through the mind… as comprehension… which creates unified thoughts with understanding between the heart and mind (wherein our soul finds contentment in oneness).

> "For out of the abundance of the heart the mouth speaks" (Matt. 12:34).

"Out of the abundance of heart" flow many thoughts through our mouth (Luke 6:45).

> "Yea, my reins [mental thoughts] shall rejoice, when thy lips speak right things" (Prov. 23:16).

> "I the Lord search the heart, I try the reins, even to give every man according to his ways, and according to the fruit of his doings" (Jer. 17:10).

The Lord governs the thoughts of man, yet man governs the heart.

Our field of faith (the ability to hear and believe) is governed by the condition of our heart. Hardened, fatty, callous, stupefied, immovable hearts deafen the mind's ability to hear truth. If this is the condition of your heart, then you may be completely unable to hear or understand spiritual truth, because once you have calloused your mind, you will harden (and perhaps completely close) your heart. Until the conditions of faith are met, some will remain spiritually deaf; therefore, at this point, repentance is essential. Conversion cannot exist without true repentance!

What Is A Hardened Heart?

During class one day, a student asked: "What is a hardened heart?" There are numerous examples found within the scriptures, so let's look at some reasons why people cannot hear His voice (Listen) which will help us understand… why people have hardened hearts:

1. A hardened heart is obstinate and rebellious toward the Lord and the kingdom of God.
2. They are more interested in building the kingdom of self and defending their opinions and religious traditions rather than believing God's truth.
3. They will put conditions on obedience to the Lord's message.

4. They will compromise the integrity of the message to make it say what they want to hear, or find it incredulous that "God would never say that."
5. They will take the word of God out of context to imply things never intended by God.
6. They are impenitent and will be unforgiving toward others, self – and God.
7. They are merciless and are more interested in holding onto an offense rather than letting it go – to grow in grace.
8. They prefer to let their past define them by rejecting God's future-based promises and what God says about them.
9. They are not interested in fairness or justice, but only in getting what they want… when and how they want it… even at the expense of others and the church.
10. They cannot embrace humility; arrogance, pompous piety and self-righteousness are badges worn upon their sleeve for all to see just how good and wonderful they are.
11. They are insensitive to the ways of the Spirit – and are insensitive to the betterment and feelings of others.
12. They are not tender-hearted. They are more concerned about gratifying self than helping others.
13. They are more concerned about how they feel versus the truth they heard. They are feeling driven… and tossed by every wave of emotion.
14. They are more interested in the superiority of their thoughts, logic and reason versus God's truth written in an ancient book long ago.
15. They are more interested in serving self and getting ahead to attain and have more… rather than serving the needs of others – and God.
16. They are more interested in justifying their sin and satisfying the flesh rather than seeking repentance from the Lord… or changing their behavior.
17. They reject the prompting of the Spirit – and the conviction of the Spirit on their heart.
18. They are more concerned about their perception of self and how others perceive them rather than reality – from God's perspective.

19. They are short-sighted on temporal gratification rather than eternal consequences; they are present-based without any plan for the future or life eternal.
20. They are more interested in mammon and the things of this world than the things of God.
21. They are stubborn; they resist change – and being transformed by the Spirit in their mind.
22. They are beholden to this world, and the love of God is not in them.

Perhaps the most intriguing aspect of the hardened heart is this: it says it wants to believe, it claims to walk in faith, but the truth is… it really doesn't believe the truth enough to listen to God's voice, be obedient to the Voice of truth, abide in truth, and walk by faith according to the truth. These persons proclaim themselves as believers in the Lord Jesus…. but they are goats wearing sheep clothing. For them, God's voice is inconvenient – and His truth onerous.

In the process of digging a firm foundation for faith, true believers will discover rocks in their soil. Goats avoid rocks, but disciples will diligently remove them because they understand… these rocks are also in their field of faith. Rocks represent anything that prevents you from growing deeper in the truth and remain obedient to Jesus. These rocks are called: "I can't" and "I won't" and they justify "I can't" with an infinite quantity of excuses. Many are the excuses of both the self-righteous and the sinful to avoid surrendering their will – completely – to Jesus.

Has the Lord hardened or closed your heart? Absolutely not! He wants to have a relationship with us; doing this would compromise His intentions.

The Lord governs the reins of man (his thoughts), but man governs his heart.

> "They have closed up their fat hearts; with their mouths they speak proudly" (Psa. 17:10).

If the condition of the heart is hard, then hearing is nearly impossible. If our hearts are hardened, then where did this hardness come from? The hardness came from the thoughts of the mind; it may have been the mind that got us into this condition to begin with, but the mind is also the instrument whereby the Spirit matures us in faith. You heard thoughts, entertained them, conceived them as reality in your mind, created a mental construct, believed them intellectually and then planted them in your heart. Once these thoughts have been believed whole-heartedly and are "planted" in your heart, the process to undo them is substantial, and for some, insurmountable! You could spend years and yes, even decades, going through counseling and psycho-analysis programs to correct stinking thinking, but the Lord in His infinite wisdom, knowing the heart and mind of man, provided us with another "one way" of escape, but this way is on His terms. The only way of escape is salvation through genuine repentance. Here is how it happens...

Our mind believes whatever it wants to believe, and then we plant these as seeds of vines of truth in our heart. Then we begin to construct fields and vineyards to increase this truth, and then we build storehouses to store the accumulated fruit of this truth. We become quite successful, so we begin to build houses to store the increase of our possessions and then more houses are built – with many, many rooms. But this is never enough, so we seek out others who are like-minded and we partner with them; now we are building a small community that will eventually become a fortified city. There simply is not enough time in the number of days that have been apportioned to us in order for us to sort through this maze in our heart and unscramble it. Our fortified cities have very thick walls, so, the only way of escape God provided is to ….

Repent!

Just let go of "you," trust, believe, repent, have faith (being persuaded and convinced), understand, receive (cling to) the truth, receive this new life as a grace gift from Christ, and then you will be given a new heart to become a new creation (born anew). At the new birth, we are given two things: a new spirit and a new heart. These are not renewed hearts or renewed spirits – they are brand new (*chadash*-2319) "in the sense of not previously existing."[47] All the garbage that we believed beforehand that was planted in our heart has now been washed away, completely removed – and is eternally gone; our new heart is iridescent snow white clean. Genuine repentance results in a turning away (from our old self-directed, corrupted ways and thoughts) – and a turning toward God (His thoughts and His ways); we must return to God by turning our heart toward Him, but only you can open what you have closed! God judges the thoughts and the intents of the heart, so He knows if you are sincere, contrite, and genuine. In this regard, you are already known by Him and will be known by Him! Even the Spirit is interceding on our behalf for our hearts to be opened, but God has given some over to a reprobate mind in order for them to come to the truth – one way or another (Rom. 1:28).

It is the will of God that our hearts be opened by the truth. And yet, there are times when we are called to pray and intercede for the lost who have "closed their eyes" to the truth (2 Kings 6:17). There are times when the Lord Himself intervenes in a person's life by sending others to open people's eyes, like the Apostle Paul (Acts 26:18); and there may be times when we are sent with opened eyes as a testimony against those who have hardened their hearts (John 9:30).

If this is you, the Lord of grace and mercy has been knocking at the door of your heart. He has been chasing after you, pursuing you, longing after you, wooing you; He loves you and wants you to remember how much He cares for you – as in the beginning. Won't you say "yes" and open the door of your heart and into enter a divine relationship with Him? How can anyone refuse such a love as this?

---

[47] Strong's Concordance. Along with this new heart and new spirit comes a new song as a response to this new saving act of God whereby our soul celebrates in newness (Isa. 42:10). This, also, is what the Psalmist writes about.

> "The Lord opens the eyes of the blind; the Lord
> raises those who are bowed down; the Lord loves
> the righteous" (Psa. 148:8).

The Lord has given us a roadmap for the healing of our heart that leads to salvation. If we have become futile in our thinking and our foolish hearts have become darkened (Rom. 1:21) then follow the steps provided in the scriptures: acknowledge the Lord, repent, convert, believe (John 17:3), be thankful and glorify God. It is that simple. Only then, can our sinful, hardened heart that has been corrupted by thoughts planted by our mind be healed (washed through repentance). Only a new heart that is governed by faith according to the Spirit is able to receive life-giving truth. But, there is one more step in the salvation/sanctification process – and this is the most critical step...

We must allow the Holy Spirit to sanctify and transform us by the renewing of our mind. If we do not allow the Holy Spirit complete access to our mind, then what do you suppose will happen? Since we were not given a new mind at the new birth, what do you think the old mind wants to do? The same mind wants to think old thoughts and plant old thoughts to return the heart to a previous state where status quo prevails. The mind will continue to plant seeds and ideas in the heart, but *what* gets planted in our field (truth or error) is predicated upon our complete surrender and submission to the Holy Spirit's prompting to renew our mind with truth. (read Regenesis, The Mind of Man, for additional help on renewing the mind by the transformational work of the Holy Spirit).

We have all believed lies, so we need to repent from the lies and replace them with truth; and when lies come at us again, we need to take every thought captive to the obedience of Christ so that we discontinue the planting of lies in our heart.

This is true salvation: the healing (*sozo*) of the mind by the washing of truth (regeneration) in the mind. Without this process, there will be no progress. Without the Spirit, there is no life.

We need a sound mind. "The 'sound' mind '*sophronismos*' (4995) means "discipline; literally, this word means saving (*sozo*) the mind through admonishing and calling to soundness of mind and to *self-control*."[48] Knowing the truth is not enough; being trained in righteousness to live according to the truth as a disciple will result in a sound mind that is obedient to God – and therefore this mind will exercise self control.[49]

Discipline for the mind (sophronismos) will produce (mathetes-3101) disciples for the Lord.

More gifted, anointed, intellectually preached and well-reasoned sermons cannot fix the heart condition of man, which is why many people chasing after teachings, revivals, prayer vigils and manifestations of His presence and His glory cannot fix the issue of our heart. We cannot keep putting patches on old wineskins and expect the anointing of the Spirit to change us and transform our rocky, hardened hearts. We need new wineskins; we need a soul that has completely surrendered the will and has received a new heart resulting from the Spirit's birthing anew process. Then – and only then – will the thoughts of our mind be able to transcend temporal reality to embrace Spirit-birthed eternity, and therefore, recognize the eternity God placed in our heart (Eccl. 3:11). We want anointing. We want revival. We want manifestations. We want the next level. We want more – but we are never able to possess or "have a share in" the glory to come until we are able to listen. Hard fatty hearts are spiritually deaf. The heart cannot have what the mind does not allow. The mind must let go – so – let God have His way in you.

Let God put His thoughts in you – by hearing His voice.

We often come to God with many words and lengthy prayer lists, but the Lord's desire for us is to listen and understand. We keep coming to Him with our needs in prayer, asking more from Him,

---

[48] Strong's Concordance.
[49] Excerpt from "Commission" section titled "The Sound Mind!!!"

like patches, a little piece of Him here and a little more of Him there when, in reality, we have already received all of Him, yet we just keep asking for little pieces from Him. We don't need more from Jesus – we just need Jesus – more! ***All we need is … more of who He is***.

> "He must increase, but I must decrease" (John the Baptist, John 3:30).

The Lord is all around us – and so is the kingdom of heaven, so why is the church settling for more program pieces and theological patches when the solution is simple: listen to what the Spirit is saying. The church needs to get back to listening, not produce more energetic sermons and sensationally loud music and announcements, petitions, collections and readings for the man show; the church needs to get quiet and listen to what the Spirit is saying – and understand!

And this is the heart condition of the church today: fat hearts and proud words! The truth comes to us through the Holy Spirit, but we have become too rigid and dogmatic in our thinking; we have become fatty, calloused and hard-hearted; we have become entrenched in our theology and we have set "pegs" down to codify our immoveable kingdom. We have reinterpreted the *rhema* and *logos* word of God so that now it is the written "Word" of God and therefore, we no longer need to listen to the voice of God or the prompting of the Spirit. Just stand on the Word, the preacher says – and then we create principles and ordinances and doctrines and traditions and platitudes in order to overcompensate for our crippled hearts. We no longer know what to think, so we trust whatever our heart is telling us, but hardened hearts cannot receive truth according to the Spirit of life in Christ Jesus. The church itself needs a heart transplant – and this must be done by the hand of the Holy Spirit whom was rejected in the first place. The church needs the mind of the Spirit, but first, it needs a new heart; otherwise, the mind of the church will return to old thoughts and old ways. See for yourself. Does the church today look anything like the first century 'new-Way' church – or does it look more like a Christianized version of 'old-way' Judaism? Open the eyes of your heart and open the ears of your mind. You know and perceive this is truth, but what on earth can we do about it? Precisely!

Wait... you didn't answer the question. Yes, I did. The question is not about what, but Who!

At the risk of eternal redundancy, it is the Spirit, the Spirit, the Spirit! Man is being transformed and renewed by one word of Christ, one thought conceived, one thought constructed, one thought planted in one fertile field at a time – by the Spirit! Likewise, the church must be reborn in the same manner. Once the Spirit begins the work of reformation and revival, the current house, known as the complacent church, will be called to repentance and the heart of the stonehouse church will be removed. A new heart that is Spirit-directed will be put in the church and then revival will begin. Let me put this as gently and yet as bluntly as necessary: the current church model needs to die. We keep creating new programs, imagine new ways to improve the church experience, change the music and tempo, preach about paradigm shifts, invigorate the message with entertainment words and theatrics to titillate the ears of the listeners, and yet, we (the people) continue to thirst and hunger for the deeper things of God. We hunger for His presence... and O, how the Holy Spirit grieves when the man-show interrupts the prompting of the Spirit. The church has a heart condition which cannot be cured with superficial solutions and hyper-managed programmatic ideas. How many more ideas and imaginative programs are we going to keep throwing at the current church model? The mind of the church cannot hear the voice of God – because the heart of the church has become hardened; indeed, it has even become calloused and seared and fatty. Faith in the Lordship of Jesus is the solid rock (not *Petros*, but *petra*) the church was established upon and built upon, as well as the faith of *all* the apostles because they listened to the Holy Spirit; yet, even they remained in Jerusalem another ten years until they were dispersed by persecution. If the church is being persecuted today, then, why do you think this is happening? Perhaps the church needs to get off its duff.

The world is craving to hear the Lord's voice and is willing to go into any church just to hear one word from the Lord and to sense His presence. The world has become desperate in its search to hear the voice of the Spirit, which is why the world no longer regards the church as the solution because they see our duplicity, hypocrisy, lethargy and complacency. By our gilded appearance, it looks real, but in reality, the church has become a voiceless tomb of religion. They have forgotten what the voice of "Who" sounds like.

The truth came to Job by way of hearing the Lord's voice and then – understanding happened. Job was a righteous man who knew "who" he was, but he did not know "why" calamity was happening to him. Much like us, Job kept inquiring of God… "Why is this happening to me?" The Lord, ever patient, loving and longsuffering, does not answer Job's complaint. And in a manner quite typical for God, He provides the answer to the question *we did not ask*, which for Job was, "Who will help you through it?" Who, indeed!

Riding a Dead Horse

The church is riding a dead horse, but the church prefers to walk in denial than to walk according to the Spirit of life in Christ Jesus. The church knows the truth, but it does not understand or comprehend or perceive the truth and more from an experiential, personal, intimate, relational way according to the Spirit. The church knows all about the river of life that flows from the Spirit, but no one can recall ever going in the river – or what the river looks like. Sadly, we prefer to read about ancient Spirit-directed saints rather than experience this for ourselves. Saturated in baptism, yes, but baptized in the Spirit… no way! Not even one drop, because that is not part of our tradition! Thus, the Spirit has been handcuffed outside to pillars supporting the church and the prophets were left chained there as well. Anathema! The Spirit is the pillar of the church!

The Father, Holy Spirit and Jesus are One, so if the Holy Spirit is chained outside the church, where do you think the Father and Son are standing? Right, again. We see this imagery clearly in the letter written "to the angel" of the church of the Laodiceans:

> "Behold, I stand at the door and knock. If anyone hears My voice and opens the door, I will come into Him and dine with Him, and he with Me" (Rev. 3:20).

This letter was written to the lukewarm, complacent, ambivalent, fatty, wealthy, lethargic church. These church members have lost their fire and have forsaken their "first love" (personal relationship) with Christ, who is now standing *outside* this door – knocking. When Christ first came to us, He called us by name with the coo of a loving whisper in our ear, but now these professed followers of Christ have shut Him out of their life; they have lost their zeal, their passion, their intimacy and, most of all, their joy. Do you see this knocking by Jesus as gentle tapping to invite them back or as the striking of the door with jealous rebuke to wake them up? And this is why many of my writings to the institutional church are stern; condemnational, no, but critical, yes! I write what I'm told to write. It is time for the bride to awaken from her slumber and answer the door – and that time is now!

> "I opened for my beloved, but my beloved had turned away and was gone" (Song of Solomon 5:6). Selah.

Jesus will not stand at the door forever. The church does not need newer programs; it needs to yearn with deep yearning and return to our first love, our Beloved Savior, and we must allow the Holy Spirit to guide us back to the open-door of truth. Without the Holy Spirit, revival is impossible, so, consider all the ways the church as tried to reinvent revival. They are much like the methods used in the story about "How To Ride a Dead Horse." (See Appendix)

The church is as organic as any human being; the church needs a new heart before revival can begin. It is not enough for the church to remember "who they are;" the church needs to remember for Whom they are – and "Who" draws them into the presence of Whom. The church without the Spirit is just institutionalized religion. It is truth imagined, yet never realized. There is an old horse according to an old covenant – but we refused to learn from observing what happened to that tradition when they refused to listen to the Spirit. He simply said one word – NEXT! The Old Covenant was rendered obsolete… and now the church is walking into the same pit of legalism, religious piety, works of service, conformity, complacency and whatnot.

The current church model needs to die. Indeed, the church age is over! The church is in transition – and a new age has already begun: the kingdom age. Are you content to be the tail of an old way or do you desire to be the head of a fresh anointing that yearns to change the world with the love of Jesus? It is time to shift atmospheres and to occupy earth with the presence of heaven in our midst as faithful hands and feet, and arms and legs… as the true body of Christ.

If you have ears to hear – and you have repented with a sincere and contrite heart – you *will* hear the voice of the Lord, so soften your heart and let Him back into your midst! Let your ears hear. Ravish the Lord with your zealous love. Listen to the Spirit. Believe – hear – and, precious bride, *live again*, as when you first believed! Indeed, leap for joy – and share your good news!

We consider ourselves the smartest generation that has ever lived on the planet, yet we are perhaps the dumbest, most spiritually deaf and disobedient fatty children our fathers have ever begotten. Regarding spiritual matters, we know much, but understand *oida* very little.

An "other" Reason

I'll tell you an "other" reason why we do not understand; "They do not know, nor do they understand; they walk about in darkness" (Psa. 82:5). When we prefer to walk in darkness, the light of truth cannot invade our spirit and we are unable to hear the voice of God. Hearing the voice of God is a spiritual discipline; it requires rigorous dedication in our search for truth. Speaking in tongues is a gift by the Holy Spirit, as are wisdom and understanding, yet understanding comes in the *mind* (*nous:* the intellect, the mind; 1 Cor. 14). Spiritual words are perceived *in* the '*nous*' mind, which is why the Spirit's work to sanctify and transform us must include the renewal of our minds – so that we can hear God's voice. (For additional information about the renewing of our mind (Rom. 12:1. 2), read Regenesis: The Mind of Man)

We are called to obedience, which means: to listen intelligently. If we were smart, we would start listening, because there are things on the spiritual horizon that have already begun to start happening, but will you have ears to know and understand what is coming?

Created To Hear God's Rhema

During the first two thousand years leading up to the Exodus, there was only *dabar* (1697) the spoken utterance word. It wasn't until Moses wrote the first five books (the Pentateuch) that we had a written word, which, by the way, Moses heard when God spoke *dabar* words to him. The prophets heard *dabar* words and wrote them as well. The apostles heard the words of Christ and wrote *rhema/dabar* words down under the direction and anointing of the Holy Spirit; then Paul began hearing *rhema* (4487) words as the Spirit spoke revelation to him, so he wrote them down as well, which has become New Covenant scriptures. Every written word we have today came as a spoken word from God, either directly from Jesus as His utterance, or the result of the Holy Spirit speaking words of truth and understanding into men in order to compose scripture and communicate *logos – the expressed heart and mind of God.* Historical events were not just documented and recorded, they were communicated under the Holy Spirit's anointing. The Bible is more than just the Word of God; these are the holy *dabar* and *rhema* words of God that were written by men who were hearing His voice – and understanding *logos* by the Spirit.

> "For this reason we also thank God without ceasing, because when you received the word (*logos*) of God which you heard from us, you welcomed it not as the word (*logos*) of men, but as it is in truth, the word (*logos*) of God, which also effectively works in you who believe" (1 Thess. 2:13).

The scriptures are not the *logos* or *rhema* words of men; they are the *logos* of God having been communicated to them through *rhema* (utterances) words of/from Christ. Exalting the Word of God above the word of God (His voice) only separates us from intimacy with the Lord that He desires. Some of us have fallen in love with a book and exalt it above all else. Anathema![50] We can hear His voice to know what His thoughts and His ways are because "we have the mind of Christ" (1 Cor. 2:16) "in whom the fullness of God dwelt" (Col. 2:9. 10). So, "let this mind be in you which was also in Christ Jesus" (Phil. 2:5) and let listening to hear His voice begin! Jesus spoke what He heard His Father say; likewise, we can speak what we hear Jesus say – and the Holy Spirit will guide us along the path of becoming listeners, play by play, but the question remains: do you want to hear? "Will" you hear God's voice? There are teachers who have instructed us that we cannot hear His voice, so I am telling you bluntly – that they are not only blind guides – they are also spiritually deaf and an offence against Christ!

Please do not misconstrue what I am saying. I am not telling anyone to stop reading the scriptures; I am able to bring this word to you with the benefit of God's word close at hand, and many other scripture-based books as well, but these ideas that I am communicating to you are not mine. I heard the Voice of the Spirit and then I searched the scriptures and meditated on them to make sure they were true messages. Believing only without listening in this age has produced many educated, well-studied, religious saints. So, then, when we hear the *rhema* voice of God, it must

---

[50] *Anathema* (331) means, "cursed yourselves with a curse." Strong's Concordance.

align with the *logos* message of God and be judged correctly by the Word of God as directed by the Holy Spirit who was sent to compose the message and guide us into all truth.

The more I read about the use and application of rhema and logos, it seems to me that they are both saying with words the truth of God; one is easily applicable and understandable with utterance words, the other as the "spirit and intent" of God's very heart and mind… therefore, revealing to us the very soul of God: His thoughts, His will and His affections (mind, will and emotion).

This requires our mind to be governed by the mind of the Spirit to comprehend spiritual truth because they are Spirit-based – as begotten in the soul (bosom) of God.

Origin and Source

> "He who does not love Me does not keep My words; and the word which you hear is not Mine but the Father's who sent Me" (John 14:24).

The Father is the Origin and Source of everything in the universe, including all messages sent through Jesus and the Holy Spirit.

"By Origin, we can say the Father is the impetus, originator, giver and source of everything whatsoever as coming *from* Him. The Origin '*ek*' denotes "the point whence motion or action proceeds,"[51] and thus, the Father is the "nourisher, protector, upholder" and Progenitor of a spiritual family for "those animated by the same spirit as Himself."[52] Our heavenly Father is the Origin of His family regarding those who walk according to the Spirit of God and have the love of God in them (1 John 4:7), and when we profess Jesus as Lord, then, by grace through faith, we are adopted into the Father's spiritual family."[53]

---

[51] Strong's Concordance, word study on '*ek*' (1537).
[52] IBID.
[53] Excerpt from "Image" section titled: "Father of the Son."

"By this verse, the Lord Jesus tells us that the spiritual words we hear belong to the Father as having come from Him. And this is what Jesus meant by in John 6:45-46[54] which could be interpreted to indicate our ability to hear the Father's voice, yet Jesus Himself tells us plainly that it is *the Spirit of the Father* that we hear." [55]

> "And the Father Himself, who sent Me, has testified of Me. *You have neither heard His voice at any time*, nor seen His form" (John 5:37).

The invisible attributes of the Father are well documented in scripture, but there seems to be some disconnect in regard to these words by Jesus. Can we hear the Father's voice? Jesus said no.[56] Over many years of reading the scriptures and hearing His voice, I have learned to take all of the Lord's words very literally – and reverently!

The Lord spoke very succinctly and He deliberately chose very specific words to convey His truth to us. ***The words came "from" the Father, yet the message came "through" Christ Jesus***. The short answer to this conundrum is: Jesus is both the Message and the Messenger… through whom the truth of God is fully expressed, revealed and manifested!

No one has seen the Father at any time – or heard His voice – yet the church spends much time and attention focusing on the Father

---

[54] (John 6: 45-46). "It is written in the prophets, 'And they shall all be taught by God.' Therefore everyone who has heard and learned from the Father comes to Me. ⁴⁶ Not that anyone has seen the Father, except He who is [παρὰ τοῦ - *with from*] God; He has seen the Father" (Verse 46 is exclusive to Jesus only).

[55] From "Image" section titled "Thoughts Beget Words."

[56] "The scriptures are very clear regarding the invisible nature of God (John 1:18; 6:46; Col. 1:15; 1 John 4:12), but this verse seems to contradict "the voice" we heard at Christ's baptism and again at His transfiguration. Bible scholars will say this verse is speaking only to those unbelieving Jews who were at Christ's baptism by John, or it refers to "the word of God" which they rejected as well, yet there is another explanation" (Read Image, section titled "Trinity Prelude.")

when we should be focusing on Jesus because… Jesus is the only True Living God this world has ever seen or heard.

There are six instances when "a voice from heaven" was recorded in the New Testament, but never does it say the voice was from "the Father." Who, then, do you suppose was speaking while Jesus was present before men with attentive ears? Jesus didn't say it and the Father didn't say it, so what's the answer? This is not a trick question, but it goes to the core problem with the institutional church that pontificates much about the Father yet refuses to hear the voice of the Holy Spirit. We need to pray to Jesus – and listen to the voice of His Spirit.

"And there also two other people groups who deliver the words of God as well: the host of heaven and the host of earth. Angels are the host of heaven and their name *'angelos'* in Greek means: messenger; and the sons of men were created as messengers for the earth as well – to declare the word of the Lord and testify of God's behalf.

"Jesus and the Holy Spirit operate in Oneness with the Father, acting in one accord, in union, in communion, in concord, in unity – being distinct yet abiding as One – in Oneness. And they declare the words of God and perform His will, to the glory of the Father.

"Regardless of our understanding or doctrinal interpretation regarding who is saying what, the Father is credited with and given honor and glory for all divinely-inspired words, which are delivered to us by Jesus and the Holy Spirit.

"When it comes to words and pattern languages, there is always a thought that precedes the utterance, and this is especially true with man as well. The Divine conversation with man and all creation originates in 'ratio' before an 'oratio' utterance, which we clearly see expressed regarding the *'logos'* and *'rhema'* of God; a Divine thought (*logos*) is followed by an utterance (spoken and unspoken *rhema* words). Within the context of creation, we see the thoughts of God to "make and orchestrate" all things according to His will and plan, whereby the manifestation of His thought is followed by all things being created and formed by the hand of Christ our Creator."[57]

"The creative thoughts of God and the creative power of His word always precede creation. In this manner, "word is two-fold: λόγος ἐνοιάθετος – word conceived; and λόγος προφόρικος – word uttered. The λόγος ὁ ἔσω and ὁ ἔξω, ratio and oratio – intelligence and utterance."[58]

"Are we able to hear God's voice? This is not a yes or no question. When we hear "the voice of God," we say this within the context of hearing a message from God through Jesus or the Holy Spirit, which is most often by thoughts and words with understanding placed within our mind. The word translated "hear" in John 5:37 is '*akouo*' and literally means: to audibly hear; but there are two main types of hearing… and then a third:

1. The sensational hearing of a sound, the sensational perception of sounds without the attentive hearing (or discerning) of the words or messages
2. The audible hearing of the message, words or thing perceived (Strong's)
3. And the third type, apart from the hearing by ears, are thoughts given with understanding into the mind of the inner man

The word-thought conceived (*logos*) precedes the word-revealed (*rhema*) manifest expression."[59]

---

[57] Excerpt from "Image" section titled: "Thoughts Beget Words" p.63.
[58] Excerpt taken from Matthew Henry's Commentary on the Whole Bible, an exposition on John 1:1; Volume VI, p. 848; MacDonald Publishing Company, McLean, Virginia.
[59] Excerpt from "Image" section titled "Thoughts Beget Words."

John 1:1

"In the beginning was Logos [the manifest presence of God's soul in all its' diversity of application and expression], *and the Logos was with God and the Logos was God"* (John 1:1).

God, our heavenly Father, is communicating Logos [His soul] to anyone who has ears to hear because we are *elohims*, created by *Elohim* to be just like *Elohim*, in the likeness of our glorious Savior, Jesus Christ. How can we refuse so great a love as this? "Why do we resist His call?"

> "This is My beloved Son, in whom I am well pleased" ... "in whom My soul delights." (Matt. 17:5; Isa. 42:1).

In like manner, as the Father's soul delighted in Jesus, so, also, the Father delights Himself in us as well when we hear His word and earnestly desire to manifest His presence.

- "Then I was beside Him as a master craftsman; and I was daily His delight, rejoicing always before Him" (Prov. 8:30).
- "He shall pray to God, and He will delight in him, he shall see His face with joy, for He restores to man His righteousness" (Job 33:26).
- "The steps of a good man are ordered by the Lord, and He delights in his way" (Psa. 37:23).

This is what the Lord promises to those who seek after Him:

> "I will put My laws in their mind and write them on their hearts; and I will be their God, and they shall be My people. ¹¹ None of them shall teach his neighbor, and none his brother, saying, 'Know the LORD,' for all shall *know* [*oida* – fully comprehend] Me, from the least of them to the greatest of them" (Heb. 8:10, 11; Jer. 31:31-34).

> "Now hope does not disappoint, because the ***love of God*** has been poured out in our hearts by the Holy Spirit who was given to us."

And, that we may know just how great His love [agape] is toward us:

> "In this the love of God was manifested toward us, that God has sent His only begotten Son into the world, that we might live through Him" (Rom. 5:5; 1 John 4:9).

His soul longs for us – He desires to "relationship" with us and tabernacle with us – and He sent *Logos*, His only begotten Son, to prove it.

Heavenly Father, "My soul delights in You." "Now therefore, I pray, if I have found grace in Your sight, show me now Your way, that I may know You and that I may find grace in Your sight" (Ex. 33:13). And I continue to pray this prayer often.

God is Spirit. God is Love. God is the intangible, invisible essence of Spirit-Love manifested in Christ, who is the tangible reality of God's Logos revealed to man in all its' manifold expressions: conscious thought conceived and intelligently conveyed; manifestations of natural wonder and glory displayed in the heavens and in the earth; mighty deeds, and the working of His will in, with and through man; the spoken word and the written word as instruments to carry His thoughts – assembled and arranged; the soul of man to willfully imitate His divine character and spiritual essence; the body of man to be a tabernacle for His presence; and the spirit in man to manifest His glory.

Who you are – is glory abiding in spirit – within an earthen vessel.

Logos Words to Hear

Jesus said to them, "If God were your Father, you would love Me, for I proceeded forth and came from God; nor have I come of Myself, but He sent Me" (John 8:42)

If *rhema* is an utterance, a spoken word (Rom. 10:17), then what is logos, if Jesus is referred to as Logos, "and the Word (Logos) was God" (John 1:1)? How can Jesus be logos 'a written word' in pre-material eternity? Well, logos must mean something other than "a written word." I do not have the fullness of understanding pertaining to the topic of "word," as I am neither a theologian nor a Hebrew/Greek scholar, so some criticism is expected – and some latitude appreciated.

"In the beginning, God created the heavens and the earth" (Gen. 1:1). At this point, the material world has yet to exist; it will be spoken into existence as a Divine utterance during the next 35 verses. The creative acts of God always begin in the mind of God, as a thought conceived, which are then transcended into material reality by the working of His will. The fullness of this working of His will resided in Christ, who is "the fullness of Godhead bodily" (Col. 2:9). Man was made (conceived in the mind of God; Gen. 1:26), then created (the actionable word uttered; Gen 1:27), and then formed of the dust (the material effect manifested; Gen. 2:7). The creative thoughts of God and the creative power of His word always precede creation.

"Word is two-fold: λόγος ένοιάθετος – word conceived; and λόγος προφόρικος – word uttered. The λόγος ὁ ἔσω and ὁ ἔξω, ratio and oratio – intelligence and utterance. There is word *conceived*, that is, *thought*, which is the first and only immediate product and conception of the soul (all the operations of which are performed by *thought*), and it is one with the soul. And thus the second person in the Trinity is called *the Word*; for He is the *first-begotten of the Father*, that eternal essential Wisdom which the Lord *possessed*, as the soul does its thought, *in the beginning of his way*, Prov. 8:22. There is nothing we are more sure of than *that we think*, yet nothing more in the dark about than *how we think*; who can declare the generation of thought in the soul?" [60]

"As a man thinks in his heart, so he is" (Psa. 23:7). Likewise, as God thinks, so it becomes.

As a man believes in his heart…mountains are lifted up and planted in the sea.

Now do you see why the Lord speaks to us as a spontaneous thought – ratio and oratio – as intelligence and utterance? The voice of God is a spontaneous thought communicated to us as a divine utterance… as thoughts in our mind. This is the righteous way that God speaks with man, in the sanctity of the divine relationship, so that we can hear His thoughts and know His ways. He is manifesting Himself, as revelation words within our inner man, within the place that no man, nation or enemy can control. This mind is now a ship of divine truth that is sailing without borders.

"The Greek noun ῥῆμα "saying, utterance, verb, word" is analyzed as consisting of the root ἐρ-/ῥε- (er-/rhe-) "say" (cf. εἴρω "I say"; ἐρῶ "I will say") and the suffix -μα (-ma), a suffix used to form nouns from verbs. In the New Testament, this noun is used in such instances as 1 Peter 1:25: "τὸ δὲ ῥῆμα Κυρίου μένει εἰς τὸν αἰῶνα" i.e. "the Lord's utterance/saying remains forever", or more commonly, "the word of the Lord endureth for ever."" [61]

Man was created "in His image" so as to hear His voice and be conformed to His likeness. Our soul, with the combined operations of heart and mind, operates within the similitude of His likeness and character for one reason: that we become like Him (Christ), as His glorious reflection and image bearers upon the earth. Our soul functions within the familiar framework of God's

---

[60] Matthew Henry's Commentary on the Whole Bible, an exposition on John 1:1; Volume VI, p. 848; MacDonald Publishing Company, McLean, Virginia.
[61] Study on 'word and rhema', source: Wikipedia.

soul, being capable of both intellect resulting in creative acts as a living soul – and – the spiritual reasoning to walk according to the Spirit as a life-giving spirit, in the similitude of Christ.

Consider these applications and similarities between how God communicates thought, and man's varied ways of expressing himself:

- A man's word is the expression of what he is thinking
- Prophecy is the expression (with words) to convey what the Lord is thinking
- You can't know a person by watching them; you must observe their "expression"
- You can't know God unless He chooses to reveal Himself to you through the Person of Jesus Christ; you can know about Him, and yet, not know His expression

The Father manifests Himself as "a God who speaks" in order to reveal Himself. This is *logos* in all variety of applications, including *rhema*. J. B. Phillips translates John 1:1 this way:

> "At the beginning God expressed himself. That personal expression, that word, was with God, and was God, and he existed with God from the beginning."

The Word (*Logos*) is Jesus Christ, who is the fullest expression of who God is, was, continually is, always being, continuous past without beginning, always being without end.

Jesus is the Potter – and we are the clay. We are earthen vessels created on purpose for a purpose – to be image bearers that reflect the image of Christ and the personification of His character abiding within us through the indwelling Spirit.

We are saints who are being sanctified so as to become a holy sanctuary, a people set apart unto God, a temple of the Holy Spirit, and a tabernacle for Christ. Let me rephrase the previous sentence by substituting a few Greek words: we are *hagios* (40) who are being *hagiasmos* (38) so as to become a *hagiasmos* (38) *hagion* (39), a people *hagiazo* (37) unto God, as a temple of the Holy Spirit and a tabernacle (permanent dwelling place) for Christ.

We are the *HAGIOS* of God. We do not need a reason… we are the reason we were created – to be *hagios*!

> "Or do you not know that your body is **the temple of the Holy Spirit** *who is* in you, whom you have from God, and you are not your own?" (1 Cor. 6:19).

> "And the Word became flesh and dwelt (tabernacled) among us, and we beheld His glory, the glory as of the only begotten of the Father, full of grace and truth" (John 1:14)

Man was created, intended, and yes, intelligently designed by Jesus, as a tabernacle for Jesus Himself. It is all about Jesus, who created everything for His Father's glory.

"For God does not dwell in houses made by human hands." Truly, I tell you –

God dwells in houses that have human hands!

"My thoughts are not your thoughts, nor are your ways My ways" (Isa. 55:8), is more of a challenge than a scathing remark by God! After all… through faith, we have the mind of Christ and we are guided by the mind of the Spirit, who transforms us by the renewing of our mind, and through the anointing of the Spirit we know all things. So, then, what is preventing us from manifesting the image, character and likeness of Jesus (who, by the way, is God)? Only one thing: hard hearts – because this prevents us from hearing His voice.

Jesus knows the Father perfectly. In Jesus, the fullness of the Godhead dwelt bodily. Jesus is heaven personified. Jesus is the Perfect Man. And Jesus wants us to imitate Him!

So, let me ask you just one question: if you want to know the truth, then who are you going to listen to? Ask Him who is the Truth! The Spirit of truth personified: Jesus only!!! And Jesus sent the Spirit of truth to guide us into all truth.

Logos, therefore, as best as I can define it is:

- "The myriad diversity and manifold expression" of revelation that God communicates to man regarding Himself being revealed in the Person of Jesus Christ, who is the express image of the Father.

"Word" has a very narrow meaning, but logos is infinite in composition of thoughts thoroughly conceived, created and conveyed. *Rhema* enables us to hear His voice, and abide in His presence, as He abides in us as Logos, the fullness of Divine expression so we can understand His thoughts and His ways. God is arranging and laying out divine truth for us so we may 'tabernacle' with Jesus abiding within us – wherein the utterance of logos is contained within a totally yielded and submitted soul that will find itself in the arms of a loving heavenly Father.

Thank you, Father, for sending Logos to us – and showing us the way back home.

"Logos is the term used by Greeks in reference to the governing power behind all things"[62] within the creative act, so let me assemble a few thoughts in the mind to see Jesus Christ as Logos. God's power and authority resides where?" At His right hand (Mark 12:36). Jesus said, "And you will see the Son of Man sitting at the right hand of the Power" (Mark 14:62). Jesus is sitting *at* the right hand of *the* Power (capital P), to whom is given

---

[62] Notes about logos, John 1:1, ESV Hebrew/Greek Study Bible; AMG Publishers.

all authority and power and dominion and strength and glory and honor and blessing? Yes, this is Jesus (Matt. 28:18; Rev. 4:11; 5:12, 13).

Logos, then, is the glorious essence of the Divine expression, as the substance of the manifest expression of God revealed *in power* through the Substance of a Perfect Man, as the revelation of God in Christ Jesus, being revealed as Logos – as the fullest living expression of God's manifest presence, power, grace and truth for mankind that we may imitate and emulate![63]

All things written, all things spoken, all types and shadows, all things created and all things manifested – exist for one purpose: to reveal the reality and identity of Jesus Christ in the fullness of His glory (John 5:37-39) as the governing power behind all things. And in all this, Jesus desires to impart to us His glory (John 17:22) that we should desire to be glory bearers and partakers of His glory.

It is all about Jesus – and God gets the glory!

May our soul (heart and mind) desire the manifest presence of God – and may our lives manifest the expressible *Logos* of God that abides in us through Jesus Christ our Lord. AMEN.

Truth Written on Heart Tablets

God is speaking to us just as He did in times before anything was written on paper; He is writing them on our hearts (Jer. 31:33; Heb. 8:10). God spoke – and His voice transformed the lives of Noah, Abraham, Moses, David and a host of many prophets – both ancient and recent. Why, then, do we have written words if God has written them spiritually on our hearts? Because we forget easily, our hearts get hardened by the cares of this world, and we oftentimes believe the lies of the enemy.

---

[63] Read "Image" for a comprehensive teaching about Jesus: the revelation of God Himself; as the Image of the invisible God.

Written words create a safety net for man to remember truth.

Furthermore, most of us have been taught that God only talked to certain individuals because He had a plan for them, as if He cherry-picked them for divine service, and that He only speaks to prophets because they have spiritual ears to hear His voice, so let me clarify something… they were not made prophets so that they could hear God's voice – they were listening and heard God's voice – and then they were called prophets. They were prophetic because they were listening. They were listeners – and so, also, are you and me. We are watchmen, seers, listeners and waiters (Hab. 2:1-3). "If you have ears to hear, let them hear" (Matt. 11:15; 13:9; 13:43; Mark 4:9, 23; 7:16; Luke 8:8; 14:33). But if we cannot hear God's voice, it is because our heart is hardened:

> "Behold the proud, his soul is not upright in him;
> but the just shall live by his faith" (Hab. 2:4).

> "Truly, this only I have found: that God made man
> upright, but they have sought out many schemes"
> (Eccl. 7:29).

The Lord desires that every nation become a nation of prophets – a people who hear His voice and do what they are told. Moses desired this for the nation Israel, but the people refused to hear His voice; "Then Moses said to him, "Are you zealous for my sake? Oh, that **all** the Lord's people were **prophets** *and* that the Lord would put His Spirit upon them!" (Num. 11:29). And Jesus is speaking this same message to everyone today:

> "My sheep *hear my voice*, and I know them, and
> they follow me" (John 10:27).

> "Pilate therefore said to Him, "Are You a king
> then?" Jesus answered, "You say rightly that I am a
> king. For this cause I was born, *and for this cause I
> have come into the world*, that I should bear witness
> to the truth. Everyone who is of the truth *hears My
> voice*." (John 18:37).

> "But He answered and said to them, "My mother and My brothers are these who *hear the word of God* and do it" (Luke 8:21; Jesus is referring to Himself, who is the Word made flesh, not the Bible)

And then we read the story about the wind and the waves obeying Jesus (Luke 8:22-25); the disciples marveled, but today, we just read in amusement. Of course the wind and waves have to obey Jesus, but for nominal Christians, our listening ability and subsequent obedience is optional. So, let me ask you this, how come the winds and waves know what His voice sounds like – but you don't? We are members of God's spiritual family when we hear His voice – and do it.

Jesus quoted the Shema (meaning: to hear – i.e. listen *and* obey):

> "Jesus answered him, "The first of all the commandments is: 'Hear, O Israel, the Lord our God, the Lord is one" (Mark 12:29; Deut. 6:4)

When Jesus was tempted in the wilderness by Satan to command stones be turned into bread, Jesus replied:

> "It is written, 'Man shall not live by bread alone, but by every *word* that proceeds from the mouth of God'" (Matt. 4:4; scripture quoted from Deut. 8:3).

Jesus said we are to live by every word that proceeds from the mouth of God. We are to hear His voice. This word is *rhema* (4487 – spoken utterance), not *logos*. This also allows us to cross-reference the Greek back to Hebrew as *dabar* (1697 – spoken utterance, word). God wants to speak to man, plain and simple, in order to reveal Himself, His kingdom and His plan of redemption to us – for us – and through us. This world is surrounded in darkness and death, and Jesus wants to talk with us as He did with Moses – "face to face," "mouth to mouth," "as a man would speak with his neighbor" and "as a friend," in clear sight and not in riddles.

The Lord Jesus wants us to hear His Voice – and obey. If we claim that we belong to Christ but we refuse to hear His voice, then we are a liar and we do not belong to Christ. If you are a follower of truth and a disciple of Christ, who is the Truth, then Jesus said you will hear His voice. You MUST hear His voice! *If* you want to hear, you *will* hear it. Period! If you do not want to hear Him, then you are not of His sheepfold. And now, anyone can answer this question: am I going to heaven?

The Father told us to "Hear Him" (i.e Jesus), the disciples taught us to hear and obey Him, the scriptures teach us to hear and understand; even the wind and waves obey His voice. So, why aren't we listening to hear His voice? It is this simple – if you want to hear, then ask Jesus to open the ears of your mind and increase your faith, but if don't want to hear, then you are free to wander around that old mountain in unbelief and rebellion as much as you want, but don't expect to see the promised land. Two generations perished in the desert because "they would not listen;" they preferred unbelief. The kingdom of heaven is for sheep that hear His voice – *and follow Him*!

> "For He is our God, and we are the people of His pasture, and the sheep of His hand. Today, **if you will hear His voice.** Do not harden your hearts, as in the rebellion, as in the day of trial in the wilderness" (Psa. 95:7, 8). "Therefore, as the Holy Spirit says: "Today, **if you will hear His voice**, do not harden your hearts as in the rebellion, in the day of trial in the wilderness" (Heb. 3:7).
>
> "While it is said: "Today, **if you will hear His voice**, do not harden your hearts as in the rebellion" (Heb. 3:15).
>
> "Again He designates a certain day, saying in David, "Today," after such a long time, as it has been said: "Today, **if you will hear His voice**, do not harden your hearts" (Heb. 4:7).

It seems the writer of Hebrews is emphatically making his point again and again (as am I): Hear His Voice! Listen to the Spirit and hear what the Spirit is saying to you.

> "He who has an ear, let him **hear what the Spirit says** to the churches" (Rev. 2:7, 11, 17, 29; 3"6, 13, 22). Selah. For such a day, as today, the Spirit's voice of revival needed for the church.

"Today, if you *will* hear His voice, do not harden your hearts." If you *will* hear – or if you won't – the choice is yours. God is everywhere, all the time, and He is in us and always talking to us, but it is we who cannot hear because either we don't want to hear, or, we already made a conscious decision never to listen. God is seeking worshippers – and He starts by finding seekers who want to hear.

"For who, having heard, rebelled?" (Heb. 3:16). Let me rephrase this question: if you haven't heard, then you are part of the rebellion.

If you have heard His voice, then your desire to live life according to the flesh in sin should begin to dissipate immediately. Hearing His voice is a working of the Spirit. Once you have heard His voice, His sweet awesome, wonderful, amazing voice, you will not want to pursue your old selfish ways – ever again. You will want to live according to the Spirit. That is just how marvelous His voice is; you will never want to compromise this ability to hear His voice again.

Once you have heard His voice and have come into His presence, you will want to hear it and experience it again and again – and you will transformed by it! *You are no longer chasing the shadow of His essence; you are experiencing the substance of His presence.* King David cried out from his soul, "Do not cast me away from Your presence, and do not take Your Holy Spirit from me" (Psa. 51:11). As a young man, David heard God's voice tell him to pick up five smooth stones to confront Goliath with a slingshot, but later in life, David made some horribly bad decisions, yet he knew what he needed most; he needed God's presence and the Holy Spirit! He needed to hear God's voice! He desired intimacy and fellowship with God.

> "He [God] raised up for them David as king, to whom also He gave testimony and said, 'I have found David the son of Jesse, a man after My own heart, who will do all My will'" (Acts 13:22).

The apostle Peter walked with Jesus, heard His voice and was the first to publically profess Jesus as "The Christ," yet when Peter was called to give an account and to testify to the truth when a servant girl confronted him after Jesus was arrested, he said, "I neither know nor understand what you are saying" (Mark 14:66-68). In this regard, many of us are also like Peter – pretending not to understand.

Listen up!!! Are we willing to pay such a high price for our spiritual infidelity?

If you hear, then you understand the truth – and you also understand what is at stake! Do you fully comprehend that a decision must be made? A verdict by you must be rendered! This is no longer a time when we can keep standing in between two ways. You have heard His voice, but will you continue to protest, "I neither know nor understand?" We all have a serious choice to make – either we believe the truth and we are going to live according to the truth – or we are denying Christ.

We have all heard His call, so, how are *you* going to respond?

You have already heard God's voice. We all have. Regardless of what you've done or what's been done to you, you have heard His guiding thoughts, but now is the moment when He is speaking directly to us – with directive words. You can still hear His voice. Everyone needs to listen and hear His voice, even if straining in deep silence to hear the faint whisper of His Voice. I promise you this: you will not die when you hear it. Some actually teach that you cannot hear God's voice and live, so read these words of truth: "Surely the LORD our God has shown us His glory and His greatness, and we have heard His voice from the midst of the fire. We have seen this day that God speaks with man; yet he *still* lives" (Deut. 5:24).

"Faith of the heart is invisible to men; obedience is of the conduct and may be observed. When a man obeys God he gives the only possible evidence that in his heart he believes God."[64]

Conversion Happens!

When we hear the living word, the voice of God, then there will be a paradigm shift; our conduct will change and our character will begin to manifest the character of Jesus.

"Those who hear will live" (John 5:25). "Hear My voice" (John 10:16). "Hear and understand (Matt. 13:23). "Follow Me" (John 10:27). "You can do all things through Christ who strengthens you" (Phil. 4:13). "I have called you to do great things" and "Greater works will you do..." (John 14:12).

> "When anyone hears the word of the kingdom, and does not understand it, then the wicked one comes and snatches away what was sown in his heart. This is he who received seed by the wayside" (Matt. 13:19).

The "wayside" has often been interpreted to mean the shoulder of the road, and in many regards this is true; however, do you cast seed on top of a road and expect any seed to germinate?

The word "wayside" is a combination of two words (*hodos*-3598; road, a route; metaphorically, a course of conduct *or* way of thinking) + (*para*-3844; alongside of, beside, near or contrary to).[65]

---

[64] Vines Expository. Word study on obey, PEITHO, number 2, paragraph 2.
[65] Strong's Concordance.

Keep in mind that this parable is about how we receive truth (in the mind) in order for a root of understanding to take effect (and grow) in our heart. The wayside represents, in one aspect, seed that is sown along one (correct) side of the road that willfully adopts the proper course and seeks this way of thinking so as to gain understanding, as opposed to the other (incorrect) side of the road that remains inattentive and obstinate thereby permitting the enemy to steal truth without allowing a root of understanding to occur. This person may accept the truth in one manner, either as factual *'ginosko'* or intellectual *'epiginosko,'* however, they will reject this truth because it is *"para"* i.e. "contrary" to the way they want, which is contrary to the *"suniemi* way" of Christ that allows understanding to occur in the heart through an open mind. Thus Satan takes advantage of this opportunity by creating doubt or fear that results in *'distazo'* (wavering between understanding and unbelief)."[66]

The "wayside" is, therefore… an alternative way "alongside of" the True Way of righteousness that results in life eternal. Within this context, I refer to religion as the "wayside" manner in which we hear truth apart from abiding in a personal relationship with Jesus Christ that compels us to become disciples. It looks good and teaches good doctrine, but it does not result in life eternal… nor does it accomplish the purposes of God on earth for which we were commissioned.

Jesus is standing at the door of your heart and He is calling to us with His voice. He is calling out to you and He is calling you by name. Jesus wants to dine (fellowship) with you and have a relationship with you, but you must be willing to listen before you can hear.

It's all about Jesus – and God gets the glory!

---

[66] Excerpt from "Understand" section titled: "Glory Revealed In Metaphors."

Oneness in Hearing

When we tune into the voice of Christ, we are no longer living as one or another, but as one unto another. We are listening in one accord because there are no denominational differences – in Christ. "Where two or more are gathered together in My name" is spoken of when two people have been reconciled into oneness of heart and mind (soul unto soul). When "sheep hear His voice," there is no longer an "us and them" mentality; we have entered into the oneness that comes by being united in the One. We are no longer goats butting heads to maintain our preconceived thoughts (prejudices), ideas, imaginations, human engineered programs and our ways (agendas and traditions); we are transformed into sheep to become the sheepfold of HIS pasture, not ours, as many sheep being lead by One, becoming one, united in oneness of the Spirit, under one Head, the Holy One of God. Follow the Shepherd. Him alone we must serve.

Once we have heard, "We must pay more careful attention, therefore, to what we have heard, so that we do not drift away" (Heb. 2:1, NIV). We must guard this truth diligently.

If you want to know who you are and what you should be doing, then ~~study~~ meditate upon the life of Jesus Christ; understand why He came, comprehend the truth – and hear Him.

We are *HAGIOS*. We are the reason we were created – to be *hagios*. Christ in us (hagios).

We are in a spiritual battle – and we are the battleground. The battle is within us – and we are the prize.

Indeed, the Word became flesh and dwelt (tabernacled) among us. The plan of God was implemented and orchestrated according to the Sovereign will of God. Nothing took God by surprise. Nothing! He knew the temptation and the fall in the Garden would happen; He knew the flood was going to happen; He knew about Abraham, Isaac and Jacob; He knew Christ would come though

Perez, the son of Judah's daughter-in-law by the seed of Judah himself; He picked a nation from among the nations, knowing they would not listen to His voice. So, do you think God was the least bit surprised when Jesus was crucified at the hands of His own chosen people?

God knew all this was going to happen since before the beginning – and that man would need a Redeemer and Savior. So, if God knew this was going to happen to His Son, then why did He allow it to happen? In a word: love. God planned for and send His only begotten Son to sons of men to show them an example of the divine nature walking in the flesh that would not glorify the flesh, but rather, would glorify the Father according to the Spirit. We would not or could not remember who we are, so the Father sent Jesus as our Divine example to show us *how* we were "intended" to live – since the beginning. Perhaps, then, we might want to remember who we are.

Jesus is the Archetype, who showed us the way – as the Heavenly Pattern to show us how to live as sojourners on earth for one season in eternity, as spiritual beings having a human experience, as image bearers sent to inhabit earth with the atmosphere of heaven within them, as sons and daughters of men being sanctified and transformed into sons of God, as dominion bearers while the earth waits, *also*, for the children of God to be revealed into the glorious inheritance as sons and daughters of God, as light bearers sent to overcome worldly darkness with the truth of Christ.

Be the light! Because darkness hates light!

The Primary Mission of Jesus

The primary mission Jesus came was to show us the way. We need to remember who we are and what we are supposed to be doing here, so He came as **"the Way"** to show us the way. His life is the template whereby we may know what the kingdom of heaven is like and how we are supposed to live. Jesus only did what He saw His heavenly Father doing – and saying what He heard His Father saying; likewise, we need to say and do what we see our King and Lord Jesus saying and doing. Our mission is the same as Christ's mission, to have dominion – under God's authority with power, so, "Let your yes be yes and Amen!"

The grace of God came under attack, so Jesus came as **the Truth** – to testify against the darkness and the kingdom of this world – and to bring order to the chaos. This is the justice of God and, through the truth, all peoples and nations and principalities and powers will be judged.

But then, man tripped over the threshold of offence that leads to sin, so Jesus came to save us from the curse of sin (death) by conquering sin and death on the cross in order that we should have **the Life** of Christ dwelling within us which saves us from eternal judgment. If Christ is not in you, then the Holy Spirit is not in you either – and the Holy Spirit is the seal of your salvation. (xx) How do you know if Christ is in you? Read 1 John – to know *if the love is in you,* or not.

Jesus said, "I am the Way and the Truth and the Life."

"For there are three that bear witness in heaven: the Father, the Word, and the Holy Spirit; and these three are one" (1 John 5:7):

1. The Father
2. The Word (Jesus Christ)
3. The Holy Spirit

The three baptisms of regeneration, which bear witness on earth and these three agree as one (1 John 5:8):

1. The water (the flood of Noah and the washing of the world with water)
2. The blood (the crucifixion of Christ; the washing away of sin with Christ's blood)
3. The Spirit (the washing of man's mind with the Word of Truth and the future coming fire when all nations will be judged; Matt. 24:36-44; Luke 17:26-30)

This is the "big-picture" gospel flying at 40,000 feet. We 'are' the purpose; we are here for a reason and our purpose – the original reason for being here – hasn't changed. Christ's original purpose for us hasn't changed. We are '*hagios*' and we here as bearers of His image, His likeness, His dominion – and to be the light of the world. And the Light came into the darkness "and the darkness did not comprehend (overcome) it." The darkness did not comprehend it and then the sons of light forgot how to comprehend it, so the Son of God came to bring *Logos* comprehension to us.

If you have ears to hear, then open your mind to the truth – and hear – then write it on your heart.

Hear, follow, obey – or please, stop pretending and just step out of the way.

> "See to it that you do not refuse Him who is speaking to you" (Heb. 12:25)

Now… let's get this reformation and revival thing moving. The appointed time has come.

> "For the vision is yet for an appointed time; but at the end it will speak, and it will not lie. Though it tarries, **wait for it**; because it will surely come, it will not tarry" (Hab. 2:3).

> "Now it shall come to pass, if you diligently obey the voice of the Lord your God, to observe carefully all His commandments which I command you today, that the Lord your God will set you high above all nations of the earth. And all these blessings shall come upon you and overtake you, because you obey the voice of the Lord your God" (Deuteronomy 28:1-2).

> "***Be still, and know*** that I am God; I will be exalted among the nations, I will be exalted in the earth!" (Psalm. 46:10).

It's all about Jesus – and God gets the glory!

Two-way Journaling

Hearing is extremely important to our personal relationship with God; it may be the only proof that we are disciples of Jesus and children of God! When we hear, it is because we are in relationship with the One who is talking to us – and we are actively listening.

Another important aspect of hearing is two-way journaling. There will come a point in time when the journaling that you are doing to record the words you hear will shift dramatically, and by this, I mean two-way journaling will happen. You are not just writing your thoughts down as you hear them, but you are also writing down God's thoughts and His answers to your questions to create dialogue. The Divine conversation has just happened!

This may begin as just a single word or small group of words, then a sentence or two initially, and then paragraphs will begin filling pages and notebooks. I already mentioned how I journaled nearly 150 pages in only a short period of time, and this is not unusual because other people I know also had this happen to them. One morning, as I was meditating on the Lord, I heard His voice and arose from bed immediately at 6:00 AM to journal… and then it happened… a Divine conversation ensued whereby two-way journaling lasted uninterrupted for eight hours straight (except for bathroom breaks). The word the Lord was speaking to me were far beyond my intellect and I still marvel at this experience (read Dominion, Chapter 14: The Lord's Dominion).

So, what is two-way journaling?

Two-way journaling is not a new concept for any disciples of Jesus: it is to be expected. In Revelation, John sees it... and as he begins to write it down, the Holy Spirit brings words with understanding to reveal what is being (or has been) observed. Some of the events are explained by the Spirit, some are explained by angels... because these heavenly visions are too incredibly fantastic to be comprehended by the natural mind of John – and us as well.

"Now..." begins a new journal entry which most likely occurred at a different time or on a different day. So now, let me ask you this: is John writing this in heaven upon heavenly paper with a heavenly pen, or is the Spirit taking Him back and forth over a period of many days to experience these events while on the island of Patmos? We really don't know; this could have happened in one day or several months because time is irrelevant in the spiritual heaven and to spiritual journaling. Is it possible to journal this much in one day? Certainly – because I have done it. When the Spirit is speaking to you and working through you, anything is possible! The yielded vessel can accomplish much in every regard and do it perfectly – as inspired text.

How you write is determined by He who dwells within you.

The Apostle Paul seems more "lumbering" when he writes, and David is more poetic. Regardless of whether you write one page or 151 Psalms, the Holy Spirit guides all "in the Spirit" to reveal His message and His truth. The inspiration of the Spirit is still navigating the thoughts of the mind and the intents of the heart to produce a word from God that is timeless across many generations and cultures. Even now, as I write, I pause moments between sentences and wait for the Spirit to bring truth with understanding. Could it happen any other way? How else could dozens of biblical writers compose script in unifying terms if not for the Holy Spirit's composition! He is the Composer and Revelator of truth to men!

In Revelation 1:9-20, John is journaling about his heavenly vision, and then he goes into "the flow of the Spirit" to begin two-way journaling (Rev. 2:1-3:22) what the Spirit is speaking to him. There is a brief intermission before Chapter 4 – and then…

… life happens. The unexpected, as well as the expected (like bathroom breaks, snacks, a knock at the door, whatever)… life happens. And then what? Refocus your thoughts like John and…

> "After these things I looked, and behold, a door standing open in heaven" (Rev. 4:1).

In John's situation, the last thing he heard the Spirit talk about was a door, so he meditated upon the last thing the Spirit said and… then he looked (with his mind) and he saw a door standing open in heaven – and then he heard a voice. This is how the Spirit works; He talks and reveals truth to willing listeners whose hearts are prepared to receive the message of truth.

And … "Then I saw" (Rev. 5:2; 7:2; 9:1; 13:1, 11; plus seven more references)

This is how it happened to psalmists, writers, teachers, preachers and apostles; they get going – and then they enter into the flow of the Spirit (or – in the Spirit) where a spiritual anointing from the Holy Spirit happens, and thus, it is no longer you doing it… it is Christ in us doing it to us through the administration of the Spirit working in us and through us. And now… give Him all the glory for it! Amen!!!

When you study the Lord's messages in the Psalms, you can see this more clearly. David is composing his thoughts and then… boom, the Holy Spirit brings the words of God while David sits with pen ready in his hand. Look closely and you might also to see the subtle cadence change when David's thoughts stop and the Lord's thoughts begin. Awesome, indeed!

The key for two-way journaling to be effective is:

Get quiet, be still, wait, listen, focus on Jesus, write something, enter into flow; interruptions will happen – so return and refocus your attention on where you left off.

Oftentimes, I have been in "flow" writing for hours at a time, and even if I had to stop to meet a friend for lunch or attend a scheduled obligation, I was able to return to flow after getting quiet and still again. There have been times when I did not want to leave the flow of the Spirit, so I called to cancel a previous engagement with "something just came up" because I would rather be in the presence of the Lord than anything else. Once you've heard the Lord's voice and you are able to hear His awesome wonderful life-giving thoughts… nothing will catch your undivided attention more than this.

God's word is timeless and eternal – even when He is speaking to you.

Grace and peace!

Patience In Silence [67]

There are times in our walk of faith with Jesus when He speaks with fresh regularity – and then there are times when there is mostly silence. At present, I am in the midst of a two-month silent period when all I can do is rest in His presence and tell Him how much I love Him, need Him, trust Him and depend upon Him for everything. I can already sense the end of this "quiet" period is coming close, not because I have heard a word from Him or anything like that, but because I can still keep my eyes focused on Him in the midst of much adversity – and – with patient endurance… remain standing.

Endurance is the most grueling part of the Christian's walk of faith; we must continue to press onward is spite of our circumstances and despite whatever happens to us. It is during these periods of time that we must learn to embrace the testing of

---

[67] Excerpt from Sojourner 12, the author's journal, dated June 11, 2016.

our faith with many trials – as well as tribulations – because the sanctification of man is critically important for God's children. We are being refined in the fire, tested, proofed, reproved, conditioned, and reconditioned again and again in order that Christ may be formed in us for one reason: to become His image and likeness upon the earth.

Anyone can believe in anything for any reason whatsoever; in fact, people who typically don't believe in something will fall for just about anything. Through faith, we are not just called to believe, as if believing in Jesus is enough… we have been commanded to believe as an act of obedience whereby we proclaim Jesus is Lord and thus, we *serve* only Him – and Him alone. Joshua 24:15 does not say, "As for me and my house, we will <u>believe</u> in the Lord," it says…

"Choose this day… as for me… we will <u>SERVE</u> the Lord" (Joshua 24:15)

Anyone can believe, yet the man or woman that professes Lordship in Jesus Christ will serve Him passionately without reservation or hesitation. For two months, I continued to serve Him faithfully according to His righteousness that is at work in me – even though I have yet to hear any substantial words from Him. I sought the Lord to see if there was any sin or separation between us; I did not hear anything, nor did the Holy Spirit convict me of sin or unrighteousness.

This period of time has been a testing of my trust in Him. You see, I have been suffering from a painful occurrence of gout (later correctly diagnosed with also a broken large toe) and contending with a broken transmission in my van (which also happens to be my place of residence). I have been in transition the past two months struggling with a thorn in my toe and no resources to fix the van. Well, two weeks ago, I began work on a deck that the Lord orchestrated to provide me with the resources I need to replace the transmission. It seems whenever I have a need (even before I know it) the Lord orchestrates the events of others in my life so that He can take care of me. We are here for a reason – to take care of each other.

And yet, there is a deeper message to this testimony: endurance is the testimony of mature saints. When I consider the first century saints like Peter and Paul who experienced many hardships and trials including martyrdom, I am encouraged to thoroughly comprehend this one thing: they were not alone… and neither are you! The Lord was watching over them, was with them and was abiding within them through every ordeal they experienced… and this is one of the blessed promises that the Lord Jesus has given us: "I will never leave you or forsake you." We may think the Lord has abandoned us or forsaken us, but we can take great solace and comfort in knowing that the Lord is abiding within us every step we take – every moment of every day. The Father was with His Son and abiding in His Son the entire time He was being beaten, scourged and crucified. Faithful ones… if Christ can endure it, then so can we. God grace is sufficient in all our needs.

Silence is not a right-of-passage for any reason that we may imagine; the Lord is simply being patient with us to see what we will do. He already knows us from the inside out, so the patient endurance of our faith is for our benefit – not His. We are the ones who need to faithfully endure every testing, trial and tribulation because our faith in Christ is being perfected so that a greater measure of His grace may be released in us – as well as through us. When our character begins to look more and like Christ (in us), then we will be activated as His ambassadors to do the greater works He promised to perform through us. Please keep in mind: the power and the authority of God in Christ Jesus do not reside in us, nor is it something that we can conjure up from within. When Jesus is Lord and is sitting on the throne of our heart, then His power and His authority is resident within us and will be released through us as we become His hands and feet to boldly speak the words of God and perform His mighty works. We are a soul abiding in an earthen vessel that has humbly submitted our will to doing the will of God – with Christ Jesus in us – doing it through us.

Consider this: all of the first century Apostles were martyred. They suffered many things: beatings, stoning, shipwreck, flogging and many other physical torments... not because God had left them; God was always with them – and within them – every moment of every day. The enemies of God in this world will do the same against anyone who walks with the Lord Jesus abiding within them, so we can take comfort in knowing that God is with us always, God is strengthening us, and God's Spirit is encouraging us to endure all things for the sake of Christ Jesus. Many believers resist the Lord of glory because of what might happen to them if they go all in, yet there is one message they have not considered: do you have any idea what you might be forfeiting if you don't? Do you have any idea what is on the other side of the eternal realm that you may be forfeiting by shrinking back from your high calling in Christ?

The church does not speak much about the mighty men and women of faith who were martyred for the name of Jesus. Yes, we read with wonder and amazement about the mighty exploits of the saints, but do we ever consider those who were martyred as a message in the Sunday sermon – and also what their greater eternal reward in Paradise will be? Did they simply die a torturous human death and are now waiting for the resurrection... or is there a special place waiting for those who left this world as a martyr in faithful obedience to Jesus Christ?

In Rev. 20:4-6, we read about those saints under the altar of God who were martyred for their faith – and these faithful ones who endured martyrdom will participate in the first resurrection of the dead to rule and reign with Christ upon the earth for a thousand years (now get this) ***never to die again.*** The writer in Hebrews talks about a better resurrection (Heb. 11:35) for those who are rewarded for service unto Jesus, but it is also very clear that those who profess faith in Christ must wait for the second resurrection when Christ will judge the living and the dead – which is after the millennial reign. And yet, we have adopted a Rapture mentality for the living and the dead that will happen before the first resurrection of the faithful in Christ because we want to be in heaven more than serving Christ with our very life – as if Jesus might be inconvenienced by us having to wait until after the millennium to be with Christ.

Not only am I willing to wait, but I am also willing to suffer and die for the sake of Christ that I may be a partaker of the first resurrection – and continue to serve my Lord and Savior on earth as much as possible. Remember what our Lord promised us in the Beatitudes for those whom are persecuted:

> "Blessed *are* those who are persecuted for righteousness' sake, for theirs is the kingdom of heaven.[11] "Blessed are you when they revile and persecute you, and say all kinds of evil against you falsely for My sake. [12] Rejoice and be exceedingly glad, *for great is your reward in heaven,* for so they persecuted the prophets who were before you" (Matt. 5:10, 11).

Our great reward is to be a member of one of three groups of people from earth who are in heaven: the chosen few (like Moses and Elijah), those who were martyred that wait under the altar and those who come out of the great tribulation (yet to occur). The martyrs will receive their reward in heaven while all others who died in Christ will need to wait until after the millennium is over to receive their reward in the resurrection. Waiting, it seems, is something we need to patiently endure in this life – and the life hereafter – until the day of Christ.

There may be silence – but we are never alone. Christ will be with us even until the end of the age. Whatever happens to us is inconsequential to who we are becoming as Christ is being formed in us… for the praise of His glory!

Listening for Spiritual Leaders (subtitled: "The Six Buts of Moses")

There have been a great many pulpit stories about Moses, the mighty man of God, with great reverence for the man regarded by Jews as their Law-giving patriarch, but there is a side to Moses that we need to see that is woven between the pages of scripture that casts a somewhat different light upon Moses – and what church leadership can learn from his mistake.

Jesus told us that we are His sheep "when we hear His voice and follow Him" (John 10:27). Jesus has been calling out to people of all tribes, creeds, nations and ethnicities so that they may hear His voice, follow after Him and walk according to the salvation that He offers, but the church has created many hurdles that prevents people from drawing closer to the Lord when He Himself says, "Come near. Do not hinder. Let them draw near unto Me."

When the Lord Jesus called out to Moses from a flame of fire within a bush, He told Moses to take off his sandals for it was holy (consecrated) ground. This is a two-fold message: when the Lord manifests Himself, it is because He has consecrated the place and memorialized the moment – and He always has good reason for its consecration. This manifestation of the Lord is reason enough for most people to approach "the talking bush" with awe and reverence.

The Lord spoke clearly to Moses, He declared His name to Moses as *YHWH*, and told him that he was being sent "to bring His people" out of Egypt (Ex. 3:10). In the first of "five buts" Moses begins to question the Lord (v.11, 13, 4:1, 10, and 13) causing the Lord to get angry with him.

- "***But*** Moses said to God, "Who *am* I that I should go to Pharaoh, and that I should bring the children of Israel out of Egypt?" (3:11)
- "and they say to me, 'What *is* His name?' [***but***] what shall I say to them?" (3:13)

- "***But*** suppose they will not believe me or listen to my voice; suppose they say, 'The LORD has not appeared to you'" (4:1)
- "Then Moses said to the LORD, "O my Lord, I *am* not eloquent, neither before nor since You have spoken to Your servant; ***but*** I *am* slow of speech and slow of tongue" (4:10)
- "***But*** he said, "O my Lord, please send by the hand of whomever else You may send" (4:13)

"So the anger of the LORD was kindled against Moses" (Ex. 4:14).

There are two aspects about Moses that we have been reluctant to discuss: his doubting questions and his disobedience. Five buts are recorded in his conversation with the Lord that constitute nothing less than doubts questioning God's word, God's sovereignty and God's authority. As we examine closely the story of the Lord's interaction with Moses, we will see a trend of inattentive listening, questions against the Lord's word and ensuing disobedience. What we need to learn from this is: when God speaks to us, then we must listen very carefully to do to all that He tells us to do – with nothing added and nothing omitted (deleted).

The Lord called Moses to be His mouthpiece to Pharaoh and also to the people of Israel. Through His words, the Lord will test Moses' obedience as the leader of His people in more ways than he might expect. Perhaps this is why Moses asked the Lord to send someone else (v.4:13) as if the Jonah approach to disobedience ever worked before. If the Lord tells you to do it, then do exactly as He tells you – because He is watching you, and others are watching and learning as well. Even his wife, Zipporah, was wise enough not to break the Lord's covenant of uncircumcision thereby testing the Lord with the life of Moses' son (v.24-26). Good for her! Way to go, girl!

On the third but, the Lord tells Moses about two of three signs that He will use to show forth His power and mighty outstretched hand if the people do not listen to his message: the rod and the leprous hand (4:2, 6); and if they still do not listen and heed the message, then use sign #4 by taking river water and pour it on dry land. It appears the third and fourth sign were never implemented, and it also appears the second sign (the rod) really got Moses and Aaron into a heap of trouble.

The Lord told Moses and Aaron to "stretch out their hand" several times – with mixed results:

- Ex. 8:6 – The Lord told Moses to tell Aaron to stretch out his hand "with the rod" to initiate the second plague, but Aaron only stretched out his hand (without the rod), which the Egyptian magicians also copied – with outstretched hands – and they also brought forth frogs like Aaron
- Ex. 8:17 – Then Aaron stretched out the rod to strike the dust so that is became lice (#3), exactly as the Lord commanded, but when the magicians tried it, they could not bring forth lice (by now, most people see a trend whereby power is being manifested by the rod, but this is not the lesson the Lord is teaching us; rather, we are to follow His word obediently – and precisely – down to the very letter)
- Ex. 9:22 – Then the Lord said to Moses, "stretch out your hand toward heaven that there may be hail (#7) in the land," but Moses stretched out the rod instead (v.23)
- Ex. 10:12 - Then the Lord said to Moses, "stretch out your hand toward the land for locusts to come upon the land" (#8), but Moses stretched out his rod instead (v.13)
- Ex. 10:21 - Then the Lord said to Moses, "stretch out your hand toward heaven that there may be darkness which may be felt" (#9) ***and so it happened!***

During the ninth plague against Egypt, the Lord told Moses to "stretch out his hand toward heaven" and thus, great darkness came over the land. No words, no rod, just stretch out the hand. Moses was faithful and he witnessed the power of God manifested in the obedient outstretching of his hand... which will come in 'handy' when they get to the Red Sea.

The Lord is teaching Moses and Aaron to obey the word (voice) of the Lord and do exactly as He commands. Period! We can observe several things happening here, but the seemingly "overlooked" disobedience of Moses in the first plague will cause the Lord to put him to the test – and at great expense to the Egyptians.

Consider and contrast this event with the rod and water – and subsequent commands by the Lord regarding 'when to speak,' 'when to stretch out the hand' and 'when to use the rod."

Moses was called by the Lord, as His proxy, to be His mouthpiece and to lift up his hand on the Lord's behalf (Ex. 6:6), but it seems Moses took matters into his own hands.

- Ex. 7:16 - Then the Lord told Moses to stand by the river and "hold the rod in your hand, and you shall say to Pharaoh, "The LORD God of the Hebrews has sent me to you, saying, "Let My people go, that they may serve Me in the wilderness"
- BUT Moses continues by adding words onto the Lord's message which did not come from the Lord... "Thus says the LORD: "By this you shall know that I *am* the LORD. Behold, I will strike the waters which *are* in the river with the rod that *is* in my hand, and they shall be turned to blood" (v.17).

Did the Lord really command this second part? Look carefully at what the Lord says next:

- Ex. 7:19 – "Then the Lord spoke to Moses, "Say to Aaron, "Take your rod and stretch out your hand over the waters" so that all the waters may become blood (but Aaron and Moses disobeyed God) "So he lifted up the rod and struck the waters" (v. 20)

The Lord is reminding Moses and Aaron exactly what to do, "to stretch out your hand," so why did they disobey God? Because they wanted to obey their own word (v.17) having thus made a bold proclamation to Pharaoh saying, "Behold, I will strike the waters..." From this one act of disobedience, the Lord sought to teach Moses and Aaron to listen carefully – and obey!

How do we know this one act (v. 17) was an act of disobedience? Because, as will we soon see, the Lord prevented Moses from walking into the Promised Land on account of similar disobedience "to obey carefully" the word of the Lord, not just once or twice, but on nearly every occasion when the Lord told him to speak only or stretch out his hand only; Moses continuously "one-upped" the Lord, as he did when he continued to question the Lord in the initial "five buts" – and in the "sixth but" to come.

We must learn this: line by line, word for word, precept upon precept – when the Lord tells you to do something, then follow it to the letter of the word! When we do anything apart from this, then we are taking His power and His authority into our own "stronghold" to do things according to our rationalized way of thinking. When we do it according to our way, then we rob God of His glory because we take the credit for what He does, *which He is still obligated to perform in order to maintain His integrity*... even though we grieve His heart by acting presumptuously.

- Ex. 14:15-26 – The Lord told Moses to divide the Red Sea by stretching out his hand (v.21, 26), which he did faithfully, but it is very important that people see this – the Lord never told Moses to stretch out the rod... but only "lift up the rod" (v.16) with his other hand. The Hollywood version teaches a contradictory message that many scripture commentators have erringly endorsed as well, that the rod parted the water when it didn't.

After the Red Sea (Sea of Reeds) was parted, the Israelites escaped and the Egyptian army was vanquished "by an outstretched hand" once again, whereby the Song of Moses was very forthright in giving this glory to God according to "His" outstretched hand:

> "Your right hand, O LORD, has become glorious in power; Your right hand, O LORD, has dashed the enemy in pieces" (Ex. 15:6).

The Lord wants to show Himself strong as our deliverer and strong tower, and sometimes He will use our hands and feet and mouths or whatever to perform what He wants to accomplish in us and through us, but when we take matters into our own hands… we violate a sacred covenantal agreement with the Lord whereby He cannot fulfill all His promises to us, such as Moses' entering the promised land. When we violate the terms and conditions of His covenant with us, the Lord is under no obligation to honor His promises to us, since the covenant was violated by our disobedience.

There have been many teachings about the voice of Moses being the primary instrument of the Lord and that the rod was a backup, but now it has become clear, however, that the voice was the primary instrument, the outstretched hand of the Lord (via Moses or Aaron) was secondary, and the rod, well, it seems yielded much power and attracted much unwarranted human reverential attention that the Lord never intended – and it got both Moses and Aaron into trouble.

The Lord does not need a rod or an instrument of any kind to demonstrate His power, but foolish humans like to use gimmicks and special effects. In this case, the rod became as an idol to Moses and Aaron in which they misplaced their trust and confidence with a flair for the dramatic, but God doesn't need theatrics… He commands obedience. We will see soon enough how the Lord put such a flagstaff rod to better use when the people complained against the Lord as they wandered around in the wilderness (Num. 21:8).

Consider now these two instances when the Lord told Moses to get water from a rock:

> "And the LORD said to Moses, "Go on before the people, and take with you some of the elders of Israel. Also <u>take in your hand your rod with which you struck the river</u>, and go. ⁶ Behold, I will stand before you there on the rock in Horeb; *and you shall strike the rock*, and water will come out of it, that the people may drink" (Ex. 17:5, 6).

Moses was commanded to strike the rock in the first instance, then speak to the rock in the second instance...

> "Then the LORD spoke to Moses, saying, ⁸ "Take the rod; you and your brother Aaron gather the congregation together. *<u>Speak to the rock before their eyes</u>*, and it will yield its water; thus you shall bring water for them out of the rock, and give drink to the congregation and their animals." ⁹ So Moses took the rod from before the LORD as He commanded him. ¹⁰ And Moses and Aaron gathered the assembly together before the rock; and he said to them, "Hear now, you rebels! Must we bring water for you out of this rock?" ¹¹ Then Moses <u>lifted his hand and struck the rock twice with his rod</u>; and water came out abundantly, and the congregation and their animals drank. ¹² Then the LORD spoke to Moses and Aaron, "***Because you did not believe Me, to hallow Me in the eyes of the children of Israel***, therefore you shall not bring this assembly into the land which I have given them" (Num. 20:7-12)

Many people cannot see the subtlety of Moses' blatant disobedience. Is there such a big difference between striking the rock the second time, or striking it twice the second time, since Moses did it that way once before? As we shall see, this was not the first time Moses did not believe and obey the Lord – word for word, but it was during this second rock-smiting event that Moses incurred the wrath of the Lord... for two reasons: 1) his actions were tantamount to unbelief that bordered on rebellion, and 2) he did not hallow (reverence) the Lord in the presence of on-looking Israelites. Moses' leadership example was disobedient whereby he allowed the Israelites to witness blatant disobedience in their leader – and God had to exact a harsh level of punishment to communicate a divine principle of unquestioned obedience by all future leaders who will be held to a higher standard of excellence, faithfulness and obedience – if these leaders want to lead "His" people.

Did Moses have a right to be angry with the people? Yes, indeed!!! But did Moses have a right to use the rod of the Lord in an unrighteous manner? Absolutely, not!

The rod was never intended to be used as a power tool by Moses or Aaron to display their position, prominence, power or authority; the rod was given as "a sign" and demonstration of God's power and presence between Moses, the man called by God, and those in unbelief to whom God sent him as a witness on the Lord's behalf. The rod was nothing more than a useless twig apart from the power of God because the power was not in the rod; rather, divine power was made manifest in 'the act of obedience' after having heard the *rhema* spoken word of God.

Whenever we use godly things, regardless of either in good ways or bad, according to our terms and understandings, we ultimately rob God of the glory He deserves. The Lord said, "My glory I will not give to another" (Isa. 42:8). Therefore, it is mission critical for the New Earth church to model obedience in this present age to carefully consider our actions to see if we are giving glory to God through Jesus Christ – or are we robbing Him of the glory He deserves.

To see the ramifications of a leader who does not operate with unquestioning faithfulness, reverence and integrity before the Lord, let's take another look at the Exodus account:

- "Then the LORD said to Moses, "Go to the people and consecrate them today and tomorrow, and let them wash their clothes. [11] And let them be ready for the third day. For on the third day the LORD will come down upon Mount Sinai *in the sight of all the people.* [12] You shall set bounds for the people all around, saying, 'Take heed to yourselves that you do not go up to the mountain or touch its base. Whoever touches the mountain shall surely be put to death" (Ex. 19:10-12).
- "And the LORD said to Moses, "Go down and warn the people, lest they break through to gaze at the LORD, and many of them perish. [22] *Also **let the priests who come near** the LORD consecrate themselves, lest the LORD break out against them" (v.21-22).

And now we shall see the sixth but of Moses:

- "***But*** Moses said to the LORD, "The people cannot come up to Mount Sinai; for You warned us, saying, 'Set bounds around the mountain and consecrate it.'" (v.23)

The Lord told Moses to keep the people back; however, this did not apply to the priests because the Lord wanted them to draw near to Him as that current generation of servant leaders who hear God's voice and model obedience in the hearing of His voice, BUT Moses countermanded the Lord's desire, as He did five times previously that resulted in the Lord's anger against him then (4:14) as well as here (19:24) when He simply said to Moses: "AWAY!"

The Lord God Almighty (Jesus) wanted Moses, "Aaron, Nadab and Abihu, and seventy of the elders of Israel" to come before Him and experience the Shekinah glory of His presence (Ex. 24:10), but sometimes even good leaders can get between the Lord and His people. The glory of the Lord "rested" on Mount Sinai ... and this is the place of permanent "rest" that Jesus has invited His followers to enter into.

Jesus wants us to enter into His presence and, through faith and obedience, consecrate ourselves as holy unto the Lord and establish a permanent abode within us for His manifest presence to abide – and His glory to rest within earthen tabernacles! The Lord's rest happens – in us – when we consecrate ourselves as tabernacles for Him to abide.

Servant leaders must take a cue from this lesson by the Lord when it comes to faithful obedience:

1. Listen earnestly to hear the Lord's voice and listen very carefully
2. Do exactly as the Lord commands – and when He says to do it, then do it
3. Do not add to or take away what the Lord tells you to do
4. Do not question His words in any manner
5. Do not compromise His words in any manner
6. Do not interpret or misinterpret the meaning of the words: just say or do as He tells you
7. Faithfully do all that He instructs you to do – and do not grow weary or anxious
8. Do not use "rods" or other symbolic things or gestures to manifest power and authority
9. Do not use the Lord's power and authority in a manner that robs Him of His glory
10. Do not get between the people and the Lord (or the Holy Spirit) as an intermediary
11. Do not prevent other servant leaders from drawing close to the Lord
12. Be very mindful that others are watching your response to the Lord's instruction
13. Teach others to listen, hear His voice, obey and follow the Lord
14. Above all, reverence the Lord and hallow Him in all your actions
15. Teach them *not* to follow any blind religious leaders who refuse to submit themselves to the sovereign Lordship of Jesus Christ in total obedience to His teachings

And teach them that Jesus wants to talk with all of us as He did with Moses – "face to face," "mouth to mouth," "as a man would speak with his neighbor" and "as a friend," in clear sight and not in riddles. Jesus wants to have a conversation with everyone that results in a divine personal relationship – with no exceptions!

This is what Moses should have taught the nation Israel… God wants to speak to them and have a personal relationship with them, but Moses acted disobediently – the people saw it – and thus, the people did not want to listen obediently either. They preferred Egypt; they preferred to complain against the Lord; and they preferred to appoint Moses as the listener who hears and intercedes on behalf of everyone. This was not God's plan, but this was their choice – and it was a very bad choice. Since they didn't want to hear the *rhema* word of God's voice, He gave them over to the written word of His voice, which came as a Law with a command: "Cursed is anyone who does not confirm all the words of this law" (Deut. 27:26). If you cannot say Amen, then say ouch!

The final chapter in the life of Moses did not end on such a sorrowful note because he is listed in the Faith Hall of Fame (Hebrew 11:23-29) whereby only one of his marvelous deeds is recorded – when he faithfully obeyed the word of the Lord in the passing through the Red Sea by an outstretched hand! How incredibly amazing! And like Moses, the final chapter of your life has yet to be written and placed within the book of remembrance (Rev. 20:12). This is something that we can learn from… rather than imitating the initial doubting, questioning and disobedient life of Moses, we can learn from the past and advance forward into faithful hearing, obedience and maturity in Christ. The Lord could not allow Moses enter into the Promised Land as a consequence for his disobedience in the presence of the people, but we see an amazing thing happen approximately 1,500 years later: Moses is present with Elijah at the transfiguration of Jesus (Matt. 17:1-8). Even though the scriptures record Moses only "ascending up a mountain" to pass from this life into the next, he is seen with Elijah the only person on earth who "went up in a whirlwind *into* heaven." How awesome and wonderful to know that Moses, the man of God, who saw the Lord face-to-face in the wilderness, was given this great honor and distinction by the same Lord he doubted, questioned, contradicted and disobeyed – yet he now lives in heaven to tell us by his own example as he stands next to Elijah – believe in the Lord Jesus and be saved. Believe every word by hearing – and *'shema'* – obey His voice.

How truly merciful, amazing and longsuffering is our wondrous Lord and savior, Jesus Christ!

Now, as we move forward, let us remove any "idols" and false pillars of faith that prevent us from living obediently to God – through the hearing of His voice. Grace and peace. Amen.

It is all about Jesus – and God gets the glory! Amen!

Appendix

25 Ways to Ride a Dead Horse

Many variations of "How to Ride a Dead Horse" have appeared, especially on the internet, and I don't know who the original author is. I've rewritten and adapted this slightly for churches, but every organization (whether it's business, government, educational institutions, etc.) can have a tendency to hold on to old forms and patterns of doing things long after their effectiveness has diminished or ceased entirely.

The tribal wisdom of the Dakota Indians—passed on from generation to generation—says that when you discover that you are riding a dead horse, the best strategy is to dismount.

Modern churches, however, have found a whole range of far more advanced strategies to use, such as:
1. Buying a stronger whip.
2. Changing riders.
3. Declaring, "God told us to ride this horse."
4. Appointing a committee to study the horse.
5. Threatening the horse with termination.
6. Proclaiming, "This is the way we've always ridden this horse."
7. Develop a training session to improve our riding ability.
8. Reminding ourselves that other churches ride this same kind of horse.
9. Determining that riders who don't stay on dead horses are lazy, lack drive, and have no ambition - then replace them.
10. Lowering the standards so that dead horses can be included and riders acknowledged with certificates of completion.
11. Reclassifying the horse as "living-impaired."
12. Hiring an outside consultant to advise on how to better ride the horse.
13. Harnessing several dead horses together to increase the speed.
14. Confessing boldly, "This horse is not dead, but alive!"

15. Providing additional funding and/or training to increase the dead horse's performance.
16. Riding the dead horse "outside the box."
17. Get the horse a Web site.
18. Killing all the other horses so the dead one doesn't stand out.
19. Taking a positive outlook – pronouncing that the dead horse doesn't have to be fed, it is less costly, carries lower overhead, and therefore contributes substantially more to the bottom line of the church's budget than do some other horses.
20. Rewriting the expected performance requirements for all horses.
21. Promoting the dead horse to a supervisory position.
22. Name the dead horse "paradigm shift" and keep riding it.
23. Riding the dead horse "smarter, not harder."
24. Stating that other horses reflect compromise, and are not from God.
25. Remembering all the good times you had while riding that horse.

[page left blank for notes]

Read the entire Image Bearer series!

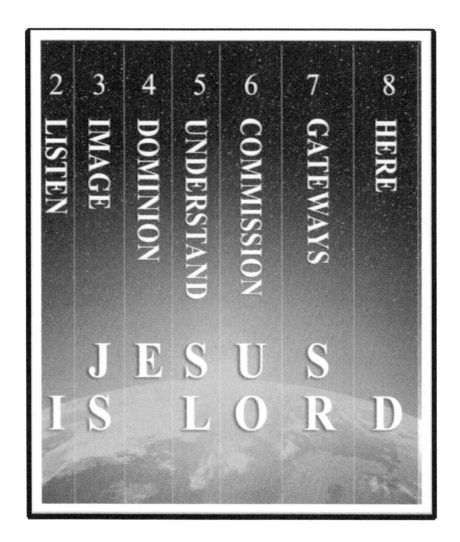

Grace and peace be yours in abundance, paul.

Made in the USA
Middletown, DE
12 November 2018